JOHN C. MAXWELL

⊨ JIM DORNAN ⊨

BECOMING
A PERSON OF
INFLUENCE

HOW *to* POSITIVELY IMPACT *the* LIVES *of* OTHERS

THOMAS NELSON
Since 1798

NASHVILLE   DALLAS   MEXICO CITY   RIO DE JANEIRO

Published in Nashville, Tennessee, by Thomas Nelson, Inc., Publishers, and distributed in Canada by Word Communications, Ltd., Richmond, British Columbia.

Nelson Business books may be purchased in bulk for educational, business, fund-raising, or sales promotional use. For information, please e-mail SpecialMarkets@ThomasNelson.com.

Scripture quotations noted NIV are taken from the HOLY BIBLE, NEW INTER-NATIONAL VERSION ®. Copyright © 1973, 1978, 1984 by International Bible Society. Used by permission of Zondervan Publishing House. All rights reserved.

Library of Congress Cataloging-in-Publication Data

Maxwell, John C., 1947–
    Becoming a person of influence : how to positively impact the lives of others / John Maxwell and Jim Dornan.
        p.   cm.
    Includes bibliographical references.
    ISBN-13: 978-0-7852-8839-8 (repak)
    ISBN 0-7852-7100-7 (hardcover)
    1. Influence (Psychology) 2. Success—Psychological aspects.
I. Dornan, Jim. II. Title.
BF774.M38 1997
158.2—dc21   97–23001
                                                                                        CIP

Printed in the United States of America

11 12 RRD 22 21 20

To all those who have been people of influence in our lives,
and especially to Eric Dornan,
whose life, experiences, and attitude
have contributed more significantly
than anything else
to Jim and Nancy's ability to positively influence people.

Contents

Preface

When the two of us met a few years ago, we sensed instantly that there was great chemistry between us, almost like that of brothers. We had so much in common—despite having very different backgrounds. Jim has spent the last thirty years in the business environment teaching people how to become successful. In the process, he built a worldwide business organization. On the other hand, John has spent the last twenty-eight years working in a nonprofit environment as a pastor, denominational executive, and motivational speaker. He is recognized as one of the top equippers in the United States in leadership and personal growth development.

What we have in common is an understanding of people and of the positive impact that one person's life can have on others. And it all boils down to one idea: influence. We know the power of influence, and we want to share it with you.

So please join us and continue reading. We're going to give you many of our insights, tell some entertaining and informative stories, and share dynamite principles that have the power to change your life—and the lives of all the people you can influence.

Acknowledgments

There are special people in our lives whose encouragement and assistance have made this book possible:

To Margaret Maxwell, whose positive support has made it possible for her husband to become a person of influence.

To Nancy Dornan, an incredible influencer to her husband, her family, and hundreds of thousands of people around the world.

To Mea Brink, for her ideas and assistance on this project.

To Stephanie Wetzel, for her proofing and editing.

To Linda Eggers, the greatest assistant any person could ever have.

To Charlie Wetzel, our writer, for his partnership on this book.

Introduction

When you were a child, what did you want to be when you grew up? Did you dream about being a famous actor or singer? How about president of the United States? Maybe you wanted to become an Olympic athlete or one of the wealthiest people in the world. We all have dreams and ambitions. Undoubtedly, you've accomplished some of yours. But no matter how successful you are now, you still have dreams and goals that are waiting to be fulfilled. And our desire is to help you realize the dreams, to help you realize your potential.

Let's start by doing a little experiment. Take a look at the following list of people. It's quite a diverse group, but they all have one thing in common. See if you can figure out what it is.

JOHN GRISHAM

GEORGE GALLUP

ROBERT E. LEE

DENNIS RODMAN

JAMES DOBSON

DAN RATHER

MADONNA

HIDEO NOMO

JERRY AND PATTY BEAUMONT

RICH DEVOS

MOTHER TERESA

BETH MEYERS

PABLO PICASSO

ADOLF HITLER

TIGER WOODS

ANTHONY BONACOURSI

ALANIS MORRISETTE

GLENN LEATHERWOOD

BILL CLINTON
JOHN WESLEY
ARNOLD SCHWARZENEGGER

---

*Influence doesn't come
to us instantaneously.
It grows by stages.*

Have you figured it out? What do they have in common? It certainly isn't their professions. The names have been drawn from lists of writers and statesmen, sports figures and artists, evangelists and dictators, actors and business professionals. Both men and women are included. Some are single and others are married. They are of various ages. And many ethnic groups and nationalities are represented. Some of the people are famous, and you probably recognize their names. But you have undoubtedly never heard of others. So what's the key? What do they all have in common? The answer is that *every one of them is a person of influence.*

Everyone Has Influence

We created this list almost at random, selecting well-known people as well as ones from our lives. You could just as easily do the same thing. We did it to make a point: Everyone is an influencer of other people. It doesn't matter who you are or what your occupation is. A politician, such as the president of the United States, has tremendous influence on hundreds of millions of people, not only in his own country but around the globe. And entertainers, such as Madonna and Arnold Schwarzenegger, often influence an entire generation of people in one or more cultures. A teacher, such as Glenn Leatherwood, who instructed John and hundreds of others boys in Sunday school, touches the lives of his own students and also indirectly influences all the people those boys grow up to influence.

But you don't have to be in a high-profile occupation to be a person of influence. In fact, if your life in any way connects with other people, you are an influencer. Everything you do at home, at church, in your job, or on the ball field has an impact on the lives of other people. American poet-philosopher Ralph Waldo Emerson said, "Every man is a hero and an oracle to somebody, and to that person, whatever he says has an enhanced value."

If your desire is to be successful or to make a positive impact on your world, you need to become a person of influence. Without influence, there is no success. For example, if you're a salesperson wanting to sell more of your product, you need to be able to influence your customers. If you're a manager, your success depends on your ability to influence your employees. If you're a coach, you can build a winning team only by influencing your players. If you're a pastor, your ability to reach people and grow your church depends on your influence with your congregation. If you want to raise a strong, healthy family, you have to be able to influence your children positively. No matter what your goals are in life or what you want to accomplish, you can achieve them faster, you can be more effective, and the contribution you make can be longer lasting if you learn how to become a person of influence.

If your life in any way connects
with other people, you are an influencer.

An amusing story about the impact of influence comes from the administration of President Calvin Coolidge. An overnight guest at the White House was having breakfast with Coolidge one morning, and he wanted to make a good impression on the president. He noticed that Coolidge, having been served his coffee, took the coffee cup, poured some of its contents into a deep saucer, and leisurely added a little bit of sugar and cream. Not wanting to breach any rules of etiquette, the visitor followed the commander in chief's lead, and he poured some of his coffee into his saucer and added sugar and cream. Then he waited for the president's next move. He was horrified to see him place the saucer on the floor for the cat. No one reported what the visitor did next.

Your Influence Is Not Equal with All People

Influence is a curious thing. Even though we have an impact on nearly everyone around us, our level of influence is not the same with everyone. To see this principle in action, try ordering around your best friend's dog the next time you visit him.

You may not have thought much about it, but you probably know instinctively which people you have great influence with and which ones you don't. For example, think of four or five people you work with. When you present an idea to them or make a suggestion, do they all respond in the same way? Of course not. One person may think all your ideas are inspired. Another may view everything you say with skepticism. (No doubt you can identify which one you have the influence with.) Yet that same skeptical person may love every single idea presented by your boss or one of your colleagues. That just shows your influence with her may not be as strong as that of someone else.

Once you start paying closer attention to people's responses to yourself and others, you'll see that people respond to one another according to their level of influence. And you'll quickly recognize how much influence you have with various people in your life. You may even notice that your influence is on many different levels in your household. If you're married and have two or more children, think about how they interact with you. One child may respond especially well to you, while another does better with your spouse. It's a matter of which parent has the greater influence with the child.

STAGES OF INFLUENCE
AND THEIR IMPACT

If you've read John's *Developing the Leader Within You,* then you probably remember the description of the five levels of leadership contained in chapter 1. Visually, it looks like this:

PERSONHOOD

PEOPLE DEVELOPMENT

PRODUCTION

PERMISSION

POSITION

Leadership (which is a specific application of influence) is at its lowest level when it is based on position only. It grows and goes to a higher level as you develop relationships with others. That's when they give you permission to lead beyond the limits of your job description. As you and your followers become more productive together in your work, then your leadership can go to level 3. And when you begin to develop people and help them reach their potential, your leadership moves up to level 4. Only a few people reach level 5, because it requires a person to spend a lifetime developing others to their highest potential.[1]

Influence functions in a similar way. It doesn't come to us instantaneously. Instead, it grows by stages. Visually, it looks something like this:

Multiply
Mentor
Motivate
Model

Let's consider each level:

Level 1: Modeling

People are first influenced by what they see. If you have children, then you've probably observed this. No matter what you *tell* your children to do, their natural inclination is to follow what they *see you doing*. For most people, if they perceive that you are positive and trustworthy and have admirable qualities, then they will seek you as an influencer in their lives. And the better they get to know you, the greater your credibility will be and the higher your influence can become—if they like what they see.

When you meet people who don't know you, at first you have no influence with them at all. If someone they trust introduces you to them and gives you an endorsement, then you can temporarily "borrow" some of that person's influence. They will assume that you are credible until they get to know you. But as soon as they have some time to observe you, you either build or bust that influence by your actions.

One interesting exception to this modeling process occurs in the case of celebrities. Because of their preoccupation with television, movies, and the media, many people are strongly influenced by others that they have never met. More often than not, they are influenced not by the actual individual, but by the image of that person. And that image may not be an accurate representation of that actress, politician, sports figure, or entertainer. Nonetheless, they admire that person and are influenced by the actions and attitudes they believe that person represents.

*You can be a model to the masses, but to go
to the higher levels of influence, you have
to work with individuals.*

Level 2: Motivating

Modeling can be a powerful influence—either positively or negatively. And it's something that can be done even from a distance. But if you want to make a really significant impact on the lives of other people, you have to do it up close. And that brings you to the second level of influence: motivating.

You become a motivational influencer when you encourage people and communicate with them on an emotional level. The process does two things: (1) It creates a bridge between you and them, and (2) it builds up their confidence and sense of self-worth. When people feel good about you and themselves during the times they're with you, then your level of influence increases significantly.

Level 3: Mentoring

When you reach the motivational level of influence with others, you can start to see a positive impact in their lives. To increase that impact and make it long-lasting, you have to move up to the next level of influence, which is mentoring.

Mentoring is pouring your life into other people and helping them reach their potential. The power of mentoring is so strong that you can actually see the lives of the persons you are influencing change before your eyes. As you give of yourself, helping them overcome obstacles in their lives and showing them how to grow personally and professionally, you help them achieve a whole new level of living. You can truly make a difference in their lives.

Level 4: Multiplying

The highest level of influence you can have in others' lives is the multiplication level. As a multiplying influencer, you help people you're influencing to become positive influencers in the lives of others and pass on not only what they have received from you, but also what they have learned and gleaned on their own. Few people ever make it to the fourth level of influence, but everyone has the potential to do so. It takes unselfishness, generosity, and commitment. It also takes time. In order to move up a level in influence with people, you have to give them more individual attention. You can be a model to the masses, but to go to the higher levels of influence, you have to work with individuals.

Bill Westafer, a friend of John's, who formerly worked at Skyline Church in San Diego, observed, "There are people whose feelings and well-being are within my influence. I will never escape that fact." That's a good concept for all of us to remember. If you lead many people or have a high-profile position, you have a greater responsibility because of your increased influence. What you say—and, more important, what you do— is a model for those who follow you. Their actions will reflect your influence.

YOUR INFLUENCE IS EITHER POSITIVE OR NEGATIVE

Now that you recognize your influence with others, you must think about how you are going to use it. You probably noticed that professional basketball player Dennis Rodman was on the list of influencers at the beginning of this introduction. Many times we've heard Dennis Rodman say that he doesn't want to be a role model. He just wants to be himself. Dennis doesn't understand (or refuses to acknowledge) that he already is a role model. It's not something he can decline. He is an example to everyone in his family, his neighbors, and the people at the neighborhood store where he shops. And because of the profession he has chosen, he is a role model to millions of others—to more people than he would be if he had chosen to be, for example, an auto mechanic. He is influencing others, and he has made a choice concerning the kind of influence he is having.

> *Even if you've had a negative effect on others*
> *in the past, you can turn that around*
> *and make your impact*
> *a positive one.*

Baseball legend Jackie Robinson noted, "A life isn't significant except for its impact on other lives." Robinson's impact on people in the United States has been incredible. In the mid-1940s, he became the first African-American athlete to play major-league baseball despite prejudice, racial taunts, abuse, and death threats. And he did it with character and dignity. Brad Herzog, author of *The Sports 100*, has identified Robinson as the most influential person in American sports history:

First, there are those who changed the way the games were played. . . . Then there are the men and women whose presence and performance forever altered the sporting scene in a fundamental manner. . . . And, finally, there are the handful of sports figures whose influence transcended the playing fields and impacted American culture. . . . Robinson, to a greater extent than anyone else, was all three types in one.[2]

Martin Luther King, Jr., one of the most influential Americans of the twentieth century, acknowledged the positive impact Jackie Robinson made on his life and the cause for which he fought. To African-American baseball pioneer Don Newcombe, King said, "You'll never know what you and Jackie and Roy [Campanella] did to make it possible to do my job."

Most of the time we recognize the influence we have on those who are closest to us in our lives—for good or ill. But sometimes we overlook the

impact we can have on other people around us. The anonymous author
of this poem probably had that in mind when he wrote,

> *My life shall touch a dozen lives before this day is done,*
> *Leave countless marks for good or ill ere sets the*
>   *evening sun,*
> *This is the wish I always wish, the prayer I always pray;*
> *Lord, may my life help other lives it touches by the way.*

As you interact with your family, your coworkers, and the clerk at the
store today, recognize that your life touches many others' lives. Certainly,
your influence on your family members is greater than that on the
strangers you meet. And if you have a high-profile occupation, you influence people you don't know. But even in your ordinary day-to-day inter-
actions with people, you make an impact. You can make the few
moments that you interact with a store clerk and a bank teller a miserable experience, or you can get them to smile and make their day. The
choice is yours.

POSITIVE INFLUENCERS ADD VALUE TO OTHER PEOPLE

As you move up to the higher levels of influence and become an active
influencer, you can begin to have a positive influence on people and add
value to their lives. That's true for any positive influencer. The baby-sitter
who reads to a child encourages him to love books and helps him become
a lifelong learner. The teacher who puts his faith, confidence, and love in
a little girl helps her to feel valued and good about herself. The boss who
delegates to her employees and gives them authority as well as responsibility enlarges their horizons and empowers them to become better workers and people. The parents who know how and when to give their
children grace help them to stay open and communicative, even during
their teenage years. All of these people add lasting value to the lives of
other people.

We don't know what kind of influence you have on others today as you read this book. Your actions may touch the lives of thousands of people. Or you may influence two or three coworkers and family members. The number of people is not what's most important. The crucial thing to remember is that your level of influence is not static. Even if you've had a negative effect on others in the past, you can turn that around and make your impact a positive one. And if your level of influence has been relatively low up to now, you can increase it and become a person of influence who helps others.

In fact, that's what this book is all about. We want to help you become a person of high influence, no matter what stage of life you're in or what you do for a living. You can have an incredibly positive impact on the lives of others. You can add tremendous value to their lives.

WHO IS ON THE INFLUENCE LIST?

Everyone could sit down and make a list of people who have added value to his or her life. We mentioned that the list at the beginning of this introduction contains the names of some people who have influenced us. Some of the names are big. For example, John considers eighteenth-century evangelist John Wesley to be a significant influence on his life and career. Wesley was a dynamic leader, preacher, and social critic. During his lifetime, he turned the Christian church in England and America upside down, and his thoughts and teachings continue to influence the way churches function and Christians believe even today. John considers Wesley to be the greatest person to have lived since the apostle Paul.

Other people named on that list are not well-known, but that in no way lessens their level of influence. For example, Jerry and Patty Beaumont had a profound impact on the lives of Jim and his wife, Nancy. Here's their story:

Nancy and I first met Jerry and Patty almost twenty-five years ago when Nancy and Patty were both pregnant. The Beaumonts were a classy couple—really sharp and confident. We were attracted to them immediately because it seemed that they really had their lives together, and we observed that they were living out their strong spiritual convictions with integrity and consistency.

Nancy met Patty one day while they were in the obstetrician's waiting room. They hit it off instantly and began to build a relationship. We had no idea how much their friendship was going to mean to us just a few months later when our lives got turned upside down.

Nancy and I think back on those days now as a good time in our lives. Our daughter, Heather, was five years old, and we were really enjoying her. We were also just beginning to build our business. It was taking a lot of time and energy to get it going, but it was fun. We were beginning to see that all our work was going to pay off in the future.

When Nancy told me that she was pregnant, I was ecstatic. It meant our little family was about to grow, and we hoped our second child would be a boy.

After nine months of routine pregnancy, Nancy gave birth to our first son, Eric. At first everything appeared to be normal. But a few hours later, the doctors discovered that Eric had been born with some very serious physical problems. His back was open and his spinal cord had not formed properly. They told us he had a condition called spina bifida. To make things worse, his spinal fluid had gotten infected during the delivery, so he was suffering from severe systemic meningitis.

Our whole life seemed to be thrown into chaos. After Nancy's hours of labor, we were exhausted and confused. They told us Eric needed brain surgery, and we had to make a decision right then. Without it, he didn't stand a chance. Even with it, things didn't look good. We cried as they prepared to take our little boy—only a few hours old—and transport him to Children's Hospital for emergency brain surgery. All we could do was pray that he would make it.

We waited for hours, but the doctors finally came out and told us Eric was going to live. We were shaken when we saw him after the surgery. We wondered how someone so small could have so many wires attached to him. The opening in his back was closed, but we could see that they had surgically implanted a shunt tube in his brain to drain off excess spinal fluid and relieve the pressure.

The first year of Eric's life was a blur for us as he repeatedly entered Children's Hospital. In the first nine months, he underwent eleven more surgeries—three of those operations came in one weekend. Things were happening so fast that we were overwhelmed, and we couldn't even comprehend what we might have to face in the future.

While we were trying to survive the midnight trips to the hospital and hold up under the pain and fear we had for Eric, guess who came alongside us and helped us survive each day as it came? Jerry and Patty Beaumont. They had come to the hospital that first day of Eric's life and given us comfort and encouragement while he was in the operating room. They brought food for us and sat with Nancy and me in hospital waiting rooms. And all the while they shared their incredible faith with us.

Most important, they helped us to believe that God had a special plan for Eric and us. "You know," Patty told Nancy one day, "you and Jim can make Eric's problems the center of everything you do, or you can use them as a launching pad for a whole new way of looking at life."

It was then that we turned a corner in our lives. We began looking beyond our circumstances and saw that there was a bigger picture. We realized God had a plan for us as well as Eric, and our faith gave us strength and peace. The Beaumonts had helped us consider and answer some of life's most important questions. From that day on, our entire attitudes changed and we had great hope.

That was more than two decades ago. Jim and Nancy lost touch with the Beaumonts, though they have since tried to find them. Now Eric has grown up and gets around pretty well in his electric wheelchair despite having experienced a stroke during one of his surgeries. He is a constant source of joy, inspiration, and humor for the Dornan family. And though their contact with Jerry and Patty Beaumont lasted only about a year, Jim and Nancy recognize the tremendous value they added to them and still consider them to be two of the greatest influencers in their lives.

Today, Jim and Nancy are people of influence. Their business has expanded into more than twenty-six countries around the world: from Eastern Europe to the Pacific, from Brazil and Argentina to mainland China. Through seminars, tapes, and videos, they impact hundreds of thousands of individuals and families each year. And their business continues to grow. But more important to them, they are sharing their strong values and faith with the people they influence. They are doing all they can to add value to the life of everyone they touch.

Recently, John was talking to Larry Dobbs. He is the president and publisher of the Dobbs Publishing Group, which produces magazines such as *Mustang Monthly, Corvette Fever,* and *Musclecar Review.* They talked about the subject of influence, and Larry shared a little bit of his story: "John, my daddy was a sharecropper, so he never had much. When he died, the only money he left me was a dollar. But he gave me so much more than that. He passed on his values to me." Then Larry said something very insightful: "The only inheritance that a man will leave that has eternal value is his influence."

We don't know exactly what your dream is in life or what kind of legacy you want to leave. But if you want to make an impact, you will have to become a man or woman capable of influencing others. There is no other way of effectively touching people's lives. And if you become a person of influence, then maybe someday when other people write down the names of those who made a difference in their lives, your name just might be on the list.

CHAPTER 1

A Person of Influence Has . . .

INTEGRITY WITH PEOPLE

MULTIPLY

MENTOR

MOTIVATE

MODEL—*Integrity*

A few years ago, while my wife, Nancy, and I were on a business trip to Europe, we celebrated her birthday in London. As her gift, I decided to take her to the Escada boutique to buy her an outfit or two.

She tried on a number of things and liked all of them. And while she was in the dressing room trying to decide which one to pick, I told the salesperson to wrap up the whole lot of it. Nancy tried to protest; she was embarrassed to buy so many things at one time, but I insisted. We both knew she'd get good use out of the clothes. Besides, she looked fabulous in everything.

A couple of days later, we took the long flight out of Heathrow Airport in London to San Francisco International Airport. After we landed, we got in line for the inevitable customs check. When they asked what we had to declare, we told them about the clothes Nancy had bought and the amount we had spent.

"What?" the agent said. "You're declaring clothes?" He read the figure that we'd written and said, "You've got to be kidding!" It's true that we had spent a little bit of money on them, but we didn't think it was *that* big a deal. "What are the clothes made of?" he asked.

That seemed like an odd question. "A bunch of different things," answered Nancy. "Wool, cotton, silk. Everything's different. There are dresses, coats, blouses, shoes, belts, accessories. Why?"

"Each kind of fabric has a different duty," he said. "I'll have to get my supervisor. I don't even know what all the different rates are. Nobody declares clothes." He looked frustrated. "Go ahead and pull everything out and sort it according to what it's made of." As we opened up our bags, he walked away and we could hear him saying to a coworker, "Bobby, you'll never believe this . . ."

It must have taken us a good forty-five minutes to sort everything out and tally up how much we'd spent on each type of item. The duty turned out to be quite a bit—about two thousand dollars. As we were putting everything back into our suitcase, the agent said, "You know what? I think I know you. Aren't you Jim Dornan?"

"Yes," I answered. "I'm sorry, have we met before?" I didn't recognize him.

"No," he said. "But I've got a friend who's in your organization. Network 21, right?"

"That's right," I said.

"I've seen your picture before. You know," the agent said, "my friend has been telling me that I'd really benefit from hooking up with your organization. But I haven't really listened. Now I'm thinking I should reconsider. He might be right after all. See, most people I see every day try to get all kinds of things through customs without paying duty, even stuff they should know better about. But you guys, you're declaring stuff you could have gotten through with no problem. That's sure a lot of money you could've saved!"

"That may be true," answered Nancy, "but I can spare the money for customs a lot more than I can spare not having a clear conscience."

As we stood in line that day, it didn't even occur to Nancy or me that anyone there might know us. If our intention had been to cheat our way through, we never would have suspected that we'd be recognized. We thought we were anonymous. And I think that is what a lot of people think as they cut corners in life. "Who will ever know?" they say to themselves. But the truth is that other people know. Your spouse, children, friends, and business associates all know. And more importantly, even if you cover your tracks really well, and they don't know what you are up to, *you do!* And you don't want to give away or sell your integrity for *any* price.

Jim's experience with the customs agent is just one small example of how people today think when it comes to integrity. Sad to say, it no longer appears to be the norm, and when confronted by an example of honest character in action, many people seem shocked. Common decency is no longer common.

GENUINE INTEGRITY IS NOT FOR SALE

You can see character issues coming up in every aspect of life. A few years ago, for example, financier Ivan Boesky openly described *greed* as "a good thing" while speaking at UCLA's business school. That flawed thinking soon got him into trouble. When his unethical practices on Wall Street came to light, he was fined $100 million and sent to prison for three years. Recently, he was reported to be ruined financially and living on alimony from his former wife.

> *The need for integrity today is perhaps as great as it has ever been. And it is absolutely essential for anyone who desires to become a person of influence.*

Government hasn't been immune to integrity issues either. The Department of Justice is prosecuting public officials as never before, and it recently boasted that it had convicted more than 1,100 in one year—a dubious record.

Just about everywhere you look, you see examples of moral breakdowns. TV preachers fall morally; mothers drown their children; professional athletes are found with drugs and prostitutes in hotel rooms. The list keeps growing. It seems that many people view integrity as an outdated idea, something expendable or no longer applicable to them in our fast-paced world. But the need for integrity today is perhaps as great as it has ever been. And it is absolutely essential for anyone who desires to become a person of influence.

In his best-selling book *The Seven Habits of Highly Effective People,* Stephen Covey wrote about the importance of integrity to a person's success:

If I try to use human influence strategies and tactics of how to get other people to do what I want, to work better, to be more motivated, to like me and each other—while my character is fundamentally flawed, marked by duplicity or insincerity—then, in the long run, I cannot be successful. My duplicity will breed distrust, and everything I do—even using so-called good human relations techniques—will be perceived as manipulative.

It simply makes no difference how good the rhetoric is or even how good the intentions are; if there is little or no trust, there is no foundation for permanent success. Only basic goodness gives life to technique.[1]

Integrity is crucial for business and personal success. A joint study conducted by the UCLA Graduate School of Management and Korn/Ferry International of New York City surveyed 1,300 senior executives. Seventy-one percent of them said that integrity was the quality most needed to succeed in business. And a study by the Center for Creative Research discovered that though many errors and obstacles can be overcome by a person who wants to rise to the top of an organization, that person is almost never able to move up in the organization if he compromises his integrity by betraying a trust.

INTEGRITY IS ABOUT THE
SMALL THINGS

As important as integrity is to your business success, it's even more critical if you want to become an influencer. It is the foundation upon which many other qualities are built, such as respect, dignity, and trust. If the foundation of integrity is weak or fundamentally flawed, then being a person of influence becomes impossible. As Cheryl Biehl points out, "One of the realities of life is that if you can't trust a person at all points, you can't truly trust him or her at any point." Even people who are able to hide their lack of integrity for a period of time will eventually experience failure, and whatever influence they have temporarily gained will disappear.

Think of integrity as having benefits similar to that of a house's foundation during a huge storm. If the foundation is sound, then it will hold up against the raging waters. But when there are cracks in the foundation, the stress of the storm deepens the cracks until eventually the foundation—and then the whole house—crumbles under the pressure.

> *Integrity is the quality most needed
> to succeed in business.*

That's why it's crucial to maintain integrity by taking care of the little things. Many people misunderstand that. They think they can do whatever they want when it comes to the small things because they believe that as long as they don't have any major lapses, they're doing well. But that's not the way it works. *Webster's New Universal Unabridged Dictionary* describes *integrity* as "adherence to moral and ethical principles; soundness of moral character; honesty." Ethical principles are not flexible. A little white lie is still a lie. Theft is theft—whether it's $1, $1,000, or $1 million. Integrity commits itself to character over personal gain, to people over things, to service over power, to principle over convenience, to the long view over the immediate.

Nineteenth-century clergyman Phillips Brooks maintained, "Character is made in the small moments of our lives." Anytime you break a moral principle, you create a small crack in the foundation of your integrity. And when times get tough, it becomes harder to act with integrity, not easier. Character isn't created in a crisis; it only comes to light. Everything you have done in the past—and everything you have neglected to do—comes to a head when you're under pressure.

Developing and maintaining integrity require constant attention. Josh Weston, chairman and CEO of Automatic Data Processing, Inc., says, "I've always tried to live with the following simple rule: Don't do what you wouldn't feel comfortable reading about in the newspapers the next day." That's a good standard all of us should keep.

INTEGRITY IS AN INSIDE JOB

One of the reasons many people struggle with integrity issues is that they tend to look outside themselves to explain any deficiencies in character. But

the development of integrity is an inside job. Take a look at the following
three truths about integrity that go against common thinking:

1.   Integrity Is Not Determined by Circumstances

Some psychologists and sociologists today tell us that many people of
poor character would not be the way they are if only they had grown up
in a different environment. Now, it's true that our upbringing and circumstances affect who we are, especially when we are young. But the
older we are, the greater the number of choices we make—for good or
bad. Two people can grow up in the same environment, even in the same
household, and one will have integrity and the other won't. Ultimately,
you are responsible for your choices. Your circumstances are as responsible for your character as a mirror is for your looks. What you see only
reflects what you are.

2.   Integrity Is Not Based on Credentials

In ancient times, brick makers, engravers, and other artisans used a
symbol to mark the things they created to show that they were the makers. The symbol that each one used was his "character." The value of the
work was in proportion to the skill with which the object was made. And
only if the quality of the work was high was the character esteemed. In
other words, the quality of the person and his work gave value to his credentials. If the work was good, so was the character. If it was bad, then
the character was viewed as poor.

The same is true for us today. Character comes from who we are. But
some people would like to be judged not by who they are, but by the titles
they have earned or the position they hold, regardless of the nature of
their character. Their desire is to influence others by the weight of their
credentials rather than the strength of their character. But credentials can
never accomplish what character can. Look at some differences between
the two:

Credentials	Character
are transient	is permanent
turn the focus to rights	keeps the focus on responsibilities
add value to only one person	adds value to many people
look to past accomplishments	builds a legacy for the future
often evoke jealousy in others	generates respect and integrity
can only get you in the door	keeps you there

No number of titles, degrees, offices, designations, awards, licenses, or other credentials can substitute for basic, honest integrity when it comes to the power of influencing others.

3. *Integrity Is Not to Be Confused with Reputation*

Some people mistakenly emphasize image or reputation. Listen to what William Hersey Davis has to say about the difference between character and its shadow, reputation:

> The circumstances amid which you live determine your reputation . . .
>> the truth you believe determines your character . . .
> Reputation is what you are supposed to be;
>> character is what you are. . . .
> Reputation is the photograph;
>> character is the face. . . .
> Reputation comes over one from without;
>> character grows up from within. . . .
> Reputation is what you have when you come to a new community;
>> character is what you have when you go away.
> Your reputation is made in a moment;
>> your character is built in a lifetime. . . .
> Your reputation is learned in an hour;
>> your character does not come to light for a year. . . .

> Reputation grows like a mushroom;
>> character lasts like eternity. . . .
> Reputation makes you rich or makes you poor;
>> character makes you happy or makes you miserable. . . .
> Reputation is what men say about you on your tombstone;
>> character is what the angels say about you before the
>>> throne of God.

Certainly, a good reputation is valuable. King Solomon of ancient Israel stated, "A good name is more desirable than great riches."[2] But a good reputation exists because it is a reflection of a person's character. If a good reputation is like gold, then having integrity is like owning the mine. Worry less about what others think, and give your attention to your inner character. D. L. Moody wrote, "If I take care of my character, my reputation will take care of itself."

If you struggle with maintaining your integrity, and you're doing all the right things on the *outside*—but you're still getting the wrong results—something is wrong and still needs to be changed on the *inside*. Look at the following questions. They may help you nail down areas that need attention.

QUESTIONS TO HELP YOU MEASURE YOUR INTEGRITY

1. How well do I treat people from whom I can gain nothing?
2. Am I transparent with others?
3. Do I role-play based on the person(s) I'm with?
4. Am I the same person when I'm in the spotlight as I am when I'm alone?
5. Do I quickly admit wrongdoing without being pressed to do so?
6. Do I put other people ahead of my personal agenda?
7. Do I have an unchanging standard for moral decisions, or do circumstances determine my choices?
8. Do I make difficult decisions, even when they have a personal cost attached to them?

9. When I have something to say about people, do I talk *to* them or *about* them?
10. Am I accountable to at least one other person for what I think, say, and do?

Don't be too quick to respond to the questions. If character development is a serious area of need in your life, your tendency may be to skim through the questions, giving answers that describe how you wish you were rather than who you actually are. Take some time to reflect on each question, honestly considering it before answering. Then work on the areas where you're having the most trouble. And remember this:

> *Many succeed momentarily by what they know;*
> *Some succeed temporarily by what they do; but*
> *Few succeed permanently by what they are.*

The road of integrity may not be the easiest one, but it's the only one that will get you where you ultimately want to go.

INTEGRITY IS YOUR BEST FRIEND

The esteemed nineteenth-century American writer Nathaniel Hawthorne offered this insight: "No man can for any considerable time wear one face to himself and another to the multitude without finally getting bewildered as to which is the true one." Anytime you compromise your integrity, you do yourself an incredible amount of damage. That's because integrity really is your best friend. It will never betray you or put you in a compromising position. It keeps your priorities right. When you're tempted to take shortcuts, it helps you stay the right course. When others criticize you unfairly, it helps you keep going and take the high road of not striking back. And when others' criticism is valid, integrity helps you to accept what they say, learn from it, and keep growing.

Abraham Lincoln once stated, "When I lay down the reins of this administration, I want to have one friend left. And that friend is inside myself." You could almost say that Lincoln's integrity was his best friend while he was in office, because he was criticized so viciously. Here is a description of what he faced as explained by Donald T. Phillips:

> Abraham Lincoln was slandered, libeled and hated perhaps more intensely than any man ever to run for the nation's highest office. . . . He was publicly called just about every name imaginable by the press of the day, including a grotesque baboon, a third-rate country lawyer who once split rails and now splits the Union, a coarse vulgar joker, a dictator, an ape, a buffoon, and others. The *Illinois State Register* labeled him "the craftiest and most dishonest politician that ever disgraced an office in America . . ." Severe and unjust criticism did not subside after Lincoln took the oath of office, nor did it come only from Southern sympathizers. It came from within the Union itself, from Congress, from some factions within the Republican party, and, initially, from within his own cabinet. As president, Lincoln learned that, no matter what he did, there were going to be people who would not be pleased.[3]

Through it all, Lincoln was a man of principle. And as Thomas Jefferson wisely said, "God grant that men of principle shall be our principal men."

INTEGRITY IS YOUR FRIENDS' BEST FRIEND

Integrity is your best friend. And it's also one of the best friends that your friends will ever have. When the people around you know that you're a person of integrity, they know that you want to influence them because of the opportunity to add value to their lives. They don't have to worry about your motives.

Recently, we saw a cartoon in the *New Yorker* that showed how difficult it can be to sort out another person's motives. Some hogs were assembled for a feeding, and a farmer was filling their trough to the brim. One hog turned to the others and asked, "Have you ever wondered *why* he's being so good to us?" A person of integrity influences others because he wants to *bring* something to the table that will benefit them—not *put* them on the table to benefit himself.

If you're a basketball fan, you probably remember Red Auerbach. He was the president and general manager of the Boston Celtics from 1967 to 1987. He truly understood how integrity adds value to others, especially when people are working together on a team. And he had a method of recruiting that was different from that of most NBA team leaders. When he reviewed a prospective player for the Celtics, his primary concern was the young man's character. While others focused almost entirely on statistics and individual performance, Auerbach wanted to know about a player's attitude. He figured that the way to win was to find players who would give their best and work for the benefit of the team. Players who had outstanding ability but whose character was weak or whose desire was to promote only themselves were not really assets.

THE BENEFIT OF INTEGRITY: TRUST

The bottom line when it comes to integrity is that it allows others to trust you. And without trust, you have nothing. Trust is the single most important factor in personal and professional relationships. It is the glue that holds people together. And it is the key to becoming a person of influence.

Trust is an increasingly rare commodity these days. People have become increasingly suspicious and skeptical. Bill Kynes expressed the feelings of a whole generation when he wrote:

We thought we could trust the *military,*
    but then came *Vietnam;*
We thought we could trust the *politicians,*
    but then came *Watergate;*
We thought we could trust the *engineers,*
    but then came the *Challenger disaster;*
We thought we could trust our *broker,*
    but then came *Black Monday;*

We thought we could trust the *preachers,*
    but then came *PTL and Jimmy Swaggart.*
So who can I trust?[4]

At one time you could assume that others would trust you until you gave them a reason not to. But today with most people, you must prove your trustworthiness first. That's what makes integrity so important if you want to become a person of influence. Trust comes from others only when you exemplify solid character.

> *Character is made in the small*
> *moments of our lives.*
> *—Phillips Brooks*

People today are desperate for leaders, but they want to be influenced only by individuals they can trust, persons of good character. If you want to become someone who can positively influence other people, you need to develop the following qualities of integrity and live them out every day:

- **Model consistency of character.** Solid trust can develop only when people can trust you *all the time.* If they never know from moment to moment what you're going to do, the relationship will never deepen to a confident level of trust.
- **Employ honest communication.** To be trustworthy, you have to be like a good musical composition; your words and music must match.
- **Value transparency.** People eventually find out about your flaws, even if you try to hide them. But if you're honest with people and admit your weaknesses, they will appreciate your honesty and integrity. And they will be able to relate to you better.
- **Exemplify humility.** People won't trust you if they see that you are driven by ego, jealousy, or the belief that you are better than they are.

- **Demonstrate your support of others.** Nothing develops or displays your character better than your desire to put others first. As our friend Zig Ziglar says, help enough other people to succeed, and you will succeed also.
- **Fulfill your promises.** Never promise anything you can't deliver. And when you say you'll do something, follow through on it. A sure way to break trust with others is to fail to fulfill your commitments.
- **Embrace an attitude of service.** We have been put on this earth not to be served, but to serve. Giving of yourself and your time to others shows that you care about them. Missionary-physician Sir Wilfred T. Grenfell held that "the service we render to others is really the rent we pay for our room on this earth." People of integrity are givers, not takers.
- **Encourage two-way participation with the people you influence.** When you live a life of integrity, people listen to you and follow you. Always remember that the goal of influence is not manipulation; it's participation. Only as you include others in your life and success do you permanently succeed.

It has been said that you don't really know people until you have observed them when they interact with a child, when the car has a flat tire, when the boss is away, and when they think no one will ever know. But people with integrity never have to worry about that. No matter where they are, who they are with, or what kind of situation they find themselves in, they are consistent and live by their principles.

THE BENEFIT OF TRUST: INFLUENCE

When you earn people's trust, you begin to earn their confidence, and that is one of the keys to influence. President Dwight D. Eisenhower expressed his opinion on the subject this way:

In order to be a leader, a man must have followers. And to have followers, a man must have their confidence. Hence, the supreme quality for a leader is unquestionably integrity. Without it, no real success is possible, no matter whether it is on a section gang, a football field, in the army, or in an office. If a man's associates find that he lacks forthright integrity, he will fail. His teachings and actions must square with each other. The first great need, therefore, is integrity and high purpose.

When people begin to trust you, your level of influence increases. And that's when you will be able to start impacting their lives. But it's also the time to be careful because power can be a dangerous thing. In most cases, those who want power probably shouldn't have it, those who enjoy it probably do so for the wrong reasons, and those who want most to hold on to it don't understand that it's only temporary. As Abraham Lincoln said, "Nearly all men can stand adversity, but if you want to test a man's character, give him power."

Few people in the world today have greater power and influence than the president of the United States. George Bush, the nation's forty-first president, had strong beliefs about power and advised, "Use power to help people. For we are given power not to advance our own purposes nor to make a great show in the world, nor a name. There is but one just use of power and it is to serve people." To keep your ambition in check and the focus of your influence on helping and serving others, periodically ask yourself this question: If the whole world followed me, would it be a better world?

BECOME A PERSON OF INTEGRITY

In the end, you can bend your actions to conform to your principles, or you can bend your principles to conform to your actions. It's a choice you have to make. If you want to become a person of influence, then you better choose the path of integrity because all other roads ultimately lead to ruin.

To become a person of integrity, you need to go back to the fundamentals. You may have to make some tough choices, but they'll be worth it.

Commit Yourself to Honesty, Reliability, and Confidentiality

Integrity begins with a specific, conscious decision. If you wait until a moment of crisis before settling your integrity issues, you set yourself up to fail. Choose today to live by a strict moral code, and determine to stick with it no matter what happens.

Decide Ahead of Time That You Don't Have a Price

President George Washington perceived that "few men have the virtue to withstand the highest bidder." Some people can be bought because they haven't settled the money issue before the moment of temptation. The best way to guard yourself against a breach in integrity is to make a decision today that you won't sell your integrity: not for power, revenge, pride, or money—any amount of money.

Major in the Minor Things

The little things make or break us. If you cross the line of your values—whether it's by an inch or by a mile—you're still out of bounds. Honesty is a habit you ingrain by doing the right thing all the time, day after day, week after week, year after year. If you consistently do what's right in the little things, you're less likely to wander off course morally or ethically.

Each Day, Do What You Should Do Before What You Want to Do

A big part of integrity is following through consistently on your responsibilities. Our friend Zig Ziglar says, "When you do the things you have to do when you have to do them, the day will come when you can do the things you want to do when you want to do them." Psychologist-philosopher William James stated the idea more strongly: "Everybody ought to do at least two things each day that he hates to do, just for the practice."

Swiss philosopher and writer Henri Frédéric Amiel maintained, "The man who has no inner life is the slave of his surroundings." *Slaves* is the right term to describe people who lack integrity because they often find themselves at the whim of their own and others' changing desires. But with integrity, you can experience freedom. Not only are you less likely to be enslaved by the stress that comes from bad choices, debt, deceptiveness, and other negative character issues, but you are free to influence others and add value to them in an incredible way. And your integrity opens the door for you to experience continued success.

It's almost impossible to overestimate the impact of integrity in the lives of people. You probably remember the Tylenol scare from years ago. Several people were poisoned to death, and investigators traced the cause to contaminated Tylenol capsules. John's friend Don Meyer sent him a commentary on the incident. Here's what it said:

> Some years earlier in their mission statement, they had a line saying they would "operate with honesty and integrity." Several weeks before the Tylenol incident, the president of Johnson and Johnson sent a memo to all presidents of divisions of the company asking if they were abiding by and if they believed in the mission statement. All of the presidents came back with an affirmative answer.
>
> Reportedly, within an hour of the Tylenol crisis, the president of the company ordered all capsules off the shelf knowing it was a $100 million decision.
>
> When reporters asked how he could decide so easily and rapidly on such a major decision, his reply was, "I was practicing what we agreed on in our mission statement."

At the bottom of the commentary, Don Meyer wrote this note: "John, it is always easy to do right when you know ahead of time what you stand for."

What's true for Johnson and Johnson is true for you and us. If you know what you stand for and act accordingly, people can trust you. You are a model of the character and consistency that other people admire and want to emulate. And you've laid a good foundation, one that makes it possible for you to become a person of positive influence in their lives.

HAVING INTEGRITY WITH PEOPLE

❏ **Commit yourself to developing strong character.** In the past, have you made it a practice to take full responsibility for your character? It's something that you need to do in order to become a person of influence. Set aside the negative experiences you have had, including difficult circumstances and people who have hurt you. Forget about your credentials or the reputation you've built over the years. Strip all that away, and look at what's left. If you don't see solid integrity in yourself, make the commitment to change today.

Read the following statement, and then sign the line below:

> *I commit myself to being a person of character. Truth, reliability, honesty, and confidentiality will be the pillars of my life. I will treat others as I expect to be treated. I will live according to the highest standards of integrity amid all of life's circumstances.*

Signature: _____ Date: _____

❏ **Do the little things.** Spend the next week carefully monitoring your character habits. Make a note to yourself each time you do any of the following:

- Don't tell the whole truth.
- Neglect to fulfill a commitment, whether it's promised or implied.
- Leave an assignment uncompleted.
- Talk about something that you might have been expected to keep in confidence.

❏ **Do what you *should* do before you do what you *want* to do.** Every day this week, find two items on your to-do list that you should do but that you have been putting off. Complete those tasks before doing anything on the list that you enjoy.

CHAPTER 2

A Person of Influence . . .

NURTURES
OTHER PEOPLE

MULTIPLY

MENTOR

MOTIVATE—*Nurture*

MODEL

Several years ago Nancy and I decided that we wanted to help our son Eric become a little more independent. Generally, he does really well. In fact, he participates in many activities that someone who does not use a wheelchair never gets to. But we thought he'd enjoy taking another step in his personal development, so we looked into something we'd heard about called Canine Companions for Independence (CCI), an organization that matches specially trained dogs to people with disabilities.

CCI has been around for about twenty years and has offices all around the country, including in Oceanside, California. That's just a short drive from San Diego, so one Saturday morning we piled into the car and went up the coast to check it out.

Eric was very excited as we got up there and toured the training facility. We met with a few staff members, and we saw a lot of great dogs. We found out that these animals spend the first year of their lives in the homes of volunteers who raise them and teach them basic obedience and socialization skills. Then the dogs are moved to a CCI center where they live and are given specialized training by staff members for the next eight months. They learn how to become working companions to just about every kind of person with disabilities other than blindness. The dogs learn how to open doors, carry objects, and do things like that. Some are trained to help people who are hearing impaired, and they learn to signal their owners when a phone or doorbell rings, a baby cries, a smoke alarm goes off, and so forth. Once a dog is fully trained, it's matched to a new owner, and the two of them go through a kind of "boot camp" to learn how to work together.

Eric loved the idea of getting a dog, and we applied to receive one that would match his needs. For the next several weeks, we waited. Not a day went by that Eric didn't talk about it. Finally, one afternoon we received a call from CCI telling us that they had a dog for Eric, and the next morning, we took off again to Oceanside.

Eric fell in love with Sable immediately. She was an energetic golden retriever who was a little over a year-and-a-half old. The two of them went through boot camp and learned how to work together. Sable could turn lights off and on for Eric, accompany him to the store with money and carry his purchases back for him, and do a bunch of other things.

As boot camp was coming to a close, one of the trainers sat down with Eric and talked with him. He said, "Eric, no matter what else you do or don't do with Sable, be sure of one thing. You have to be the one who feeds her. That's very important. It's the only way to be sure that she will bond with you and look to you as her master."

For Eric, giving the dog love and affection was easy. He enjoyed petting and grooming her, but it was harder for him to learn how to take charge. He has a pretty docile personality. But in time, he learned to feed her, and it eventually became his favorite part of their routine.

Feeding a dog is the best way to create a relationship with her. It not only provides what the dog needs, giving her life and strength, but it also teaches her to trust and follow you. And in most cases, when you do the feeding, the care you give is returned with loyalty, obedience, and affection.

The Nature of Nurture

In some regards, people respond similarly to the way some animals do. Like animals, people need to be cared for, not just physically, but emotionally. If you look around, you'll discover that there are people in your life who want to be fed—with encouragement, recognition, security, and hope. That process is called nurturing, and it's a need of every human being.

If you desire to become an influencer in others' lives, start by nurturing them. Many people mistakenly believe that the way to become an influencer is to become an authority figure—correct others' errors, reveal the weak areas they can't easily see in themselves, and give so-called constructive criticism. But what clergyman John Knox said more than four hundred years ago is still true: "You cannot antagonize and influence at the same time."

At the heart of the nurturing process is genuine concern for others. When you hear the word *nurture,* what do you first think of? If you're like most people, you probably envision a mother cradling a baby. She takes care of her child, protecting him, feeding him, encouraging him, making sure that his needs are met. She doesn't give him attention only when she has spare time or when it's convenient. She loves him and wants him to thrive. Similarly, as you try to help and influence the people around you, you must have positive feelings and concern for them. If you want to make a positive impact on them, you cannot dislike, despise, or disparage them. You must give them love and respect. Or as human relations expert Les Giblin put it, "You can't make the other fellow feel important in your presence if you secretly feel that he is a nobody."

*If you nurture others but allow them to become
dependent on you, you're really hurting them,
not helping them.*

You may be wondering why you should take on a nurturing role with the people you want to influence, especially if they are employees, colleagues, or friends—not family members. You may be saying to yourself, Isn't that something they can get somewhere else, for example, at home? The unfortunate truth is that most people are desperate for encouragement. And even if a few people in their lives build them up, you still need to become a nurturer to them because people are influenced most by those who make them feel the best about themselves. If you become a major nurturer in the lives of others, then you have an opportunity to make a major impact on them.

Check and recheck your motives as you help and encourage others. Don't be like a little girl named Emily. Her father, Guy Belleranti, was driving the family home from church one Sunday when the five-year-old girl said, "When I grow up, I want to be like the man who stood in front."

"You want to be a minister?" asked Emily's mother.

"No," said Emily, "I want to tell people what to do."

Your goal is others' growth and independence. If you nurture others but allow them to become dependent on you, you're really hurting them, not helping them. And if you help them because of your desire to meet your needs or to heal the hurts of your past, your relationship with them can become codependent. It's not healthy to try to correct your personal history by reliving it vicariously through others. Besides, codependent people never become positive influencers in the lives of others.

A Nurturing Influencer Is a Giver

Now that you have a better idea about what it means to nurture others, you're probably ready to learn how to do it with the people in your life: employees, family members, friends, fellow church workers, and colleagues. You do it by focusing on *giving* rather than *getting*. Start by giving to others in these areas:

Love

Before you can do anything else in the lives of others, you must show them love. Without it, there can be no connection, no future, and no success together. Think back to some key people who have had an impact on your life: an incredible teacher, a fantastic boss, a special aunt or uncle. Undoubtedly, when you spent time with those people, you could sense that they cared about you. And in return, you responded positively to them.

We discovered this example of how love can make a difference in the lives of students. Here is something written by a thoughtful teacher:

> I had a great feeling of relief when I began to understand that a young-
> ster needs more than just subject matter. I know mathematics well, and
> I teach it well. I used to think that was all I needed to do. Now I teach
> children, not math. I accept the fact that I can only succeed partially
> with some of them. When I don't have to know all the answers, I seem
> to have more answers than when I tried to be the expert. The young-

ster who really made me understand this was Eddie. I asked him one day why he thought he was doing so much better than last year. He gave meaning to my whole new orientation. "It's because I like myself now when I'm with you," he said.[1]

Eddie responded to love in a way that he never would have to knowledge, psychology, technique, or educational theory. When he knew his teacher cared about him, he blossomed.

> *Without love, there can be no connection,*
> *no future, and no success together.*

The length and breadth of our influence on others are directly related to the depth of our concern for them. When it comes to helping people grow and feel good about themselves, there is no substitute for love. Even a tough guy like Vince Lombardi, the legendary coach of the Green Bay Packers, understood the power of love to bring out people's best and make an impact on their lives. He said, "There are a lot of coaches with good ball clubs who know the fundamentals and have plenty of discipline but still don't win the game. Then you come to the third ingredient: If you're going to play together as a team, you've got to care for one another. You've got to *love* each other. Each player has to be thinking about the next guy."

You can positively impact people by nurturing them. It doesn't matter what profession you're in. And it doesn't matter how successful the people around you are or what they have accomplished in the past. Everyone needs to feel valued. Even someone who was once the leader of the free world needs love. In his book *In the Arena,* former president Richard Nixon described his depression following his resignation from the White House and his undergoing surgery. At one point when he was in the hospital, he told his wife, Pat, that he wanted to die.

When he was at the absolute lowest point in his life, a nurse in the hospital came into his room, opened the drapes, and pointed out a small plane that was flying back and forth overhead. It was pulling this sign:

GOD LOVES YOU, AND SO DO WE. Ruth Graham, evangelist Billy Graham's wife, had arranged for the plane to fly by the hospital. That's when Nixon experienced a turning point. Seeing that expression of love gave him the courage and desire to keep going and recover.

Take time to express your love and appreciation for the people close to you. Tell them how much they mean to you. Write them notes telling how much you care. Give them a pat on the back and, when appropriate, a hug. Don't ever assume that people know how you feel about them. Tell them. Nobody can be told too often that he or she is loved.

Respect

We read a story about a woman who moved to a small town. After being there a short time, she complained to her neighbor about the poor service she received at the local drugstore. She was hoping her new acquaintance would repeat her criticism to the store's owner.

The next time the newcomer went to the drugstore, the druggist greeted her with a big smile, told her how happy he was to see her again, and said he hoped she liked their town. He also offered himself as a resource to the woman and her husband as they got settled. Then he took care of her order quickly and efficiently.

Later the woman reported the incredible change to her friend. "I suppose you told him how poor I thought the service was?" she declared.

"Well, no," the neighbor said. "In fact—and I hope you don't mind—I told him you were amazed at the way he had built up this small town drugstore, and that you thought it was one of the best-run drugstores you'd ever seen."[2]

That woman's neighbor understood that people respond to respect. In fact, most people will do nearly anything for you if you treat them respectfully. That means making it clear to them that their feelings are important, their preferences are respected, and their opinions are valuable. It means giving them the benefit of the doubt. Or as philosopher-poet Ralph Waldo Emerson put it, "Every man is entitled to be valued by his best moments."

Where love focuses on giving to others, respect shows a willingness to receive from them. Respect acknowledges another person's ability or potential to contribute. Listening to other people and putting their agenda ahead of your own reflect your respect for them and have the potential to make you and them more successful. According to a recent study by Teleometrics International reported in the *Wall Street Journal,* executives understand the power of respect. Among the sixteen thousand executives surveyed, the researchers concentrated on a group of high achievers. Within that group, all had positive attitudes about their subordinates, frequently sought their advice, regularly listened to their concerns, and treated them with respect.

If you have had the opportunity to work in many environments, and you have worked for both types of people—those who *have* and those who *have not* shown you respect—you understand how motivational respect can be. And you also know that you are more easily influenced by people who treat you well.

Sense of Security

Another important part of nurturing is giving people a sense of security. People are reluctant to trust you and reach their potential when they are worried about whether they're safe with you. But when they feel secure, they are in a position to respond positively and do their best. Virginia Arcastle remarked, "When people are made to feel secure and important and appreciated, it will no longer be necessary for them to whittle down others in order to seem bigger in comparison."

Part of making people feel secure comes from integrity, which we talked about in the previous chapter. People feel secure with you when your actions and words are consistent and conform to a high moral code that includes respect. Former Notre Dame head football coach Lou Holtz addressed that issue when he said, "Do what's right! Do the best you can and treat others the way you want to be treated because they will ask three questions: (1) Can I trust you? (2) Are you committed? . . . (3) Do you care about me as a person?"

People desire security not only from you but also from their environment. Good leaders recognize this and create an environment where people can flourish. Mike Krzyzewski, successful head basketball coach of Duke University, understands the impact a leader can make when he provides security to the people who follow him: "If you set up an atmosphere of communication and trust, it becomes a tradition. Older team members will establish your credibility with newer ones. Even if they don't like everything about you, they'll still say, 'He's trustworthy, committed to us as a team.'"

Not until people can completely trust you will you be able to positively influence them and have an impact on their lives.

Recognition

A too common mistake, especially among leaders in the marketplace, is failure to share recognition and show appreciation to others. For example, J. C. Staehle did an analysis of workers in America and found that the number one cause of dissatisfaction among employees was their superiors' failure to give them credit. It's difficult for people to follow someone who doesn't appreciate them for who they are and what they do. As former secretary of defense and World Bank president Robert McNamara said, "Brains are like hearts—they go where they are appreciated."

Recognition is greatly appreciated by everyone, not just people in business and industry. Even a little bit of recognition can go an incredibly long way in a person's life. For example, we recently read a story written by Helen P. Mrosla, a teaching nun. She told about her experience with Mark Eklund, a student she had taught in third grade and then again in junior high math. Here's her story:

> One Friday [in the classroom] things just didn't feel right. We had worked hard on a new concept all week, and I sensed that the students were growing frustrated with themselves—and edgy with one another. I had to stop this crankiness before it got out of hand. So I asked them to list the names of the other students in the room on two sheets of paper, leaving a space between each name. Then I told them to think of the nicest thing they could say about each of their classmates and write it down.

It took the remainder of the class period to finish the assignment, but as the students left the room, each one handed me their paper. . . .

That Saturday, I wrote down the name of each student on a separate sheet of paper, and I listed what everyone else had said about that individual. On Monday I gave each student his or her list. Some of them ran two pages. Before long, the entire class was smiling. "Really?" I heard whispered. "I never knew that meant anything to anyone!" "I didn't know others liked me so much!"

No one ever mentioned those papers in class again. I never knew if they discussed them after class or with their parents, but it didn't matter. The exercise had accomplished its purpose. The students were happy with themselves and one another again.

That group of students moved on. Several years later, after I had returned from a vacation, my parents met me at the airport. As we were driving home, Mother asked the usual questions about the trip: How the weather was, my experiences in general. There was a slight lull in the conversation. Mother gave Dad a sideways glance and simply said, "Dad?" My father cleared his throat. "The Eklunds called last night," he began.

"Really?" I said. "I haven't heard from them for several years. I wonder how Mark is."

Dad responded quietly. "Mark was killed in Vietnam," he said. "The funeral is tomorrow, and his parents would like it if you could attend." To this day I can still point to the exact spot on I-494 where Dad told me about Mark.

I had never seen a serviceman in a military coffin before. . . . The church was packed with Mark's friends. [His old classmate] Chuck's sister sang "The Battle Hymn of the Republic." Why did it have to rain on the day of the funeral? It was difficult enough at the grave side. The pastor said the usual prayers and the bugler played taps. One by one those who loved Mark took a last walk by the coffin and sprinkled it with holy water.

I was the last one to bless the coffin. As I stood there, one of the soldiers who had acted as a pallbearer came up to me. "Were you Mark's math teacher?" he asked. I nodded as I continued to stare at the coffin. "Mark talked about you a lot," he said.

After the funeral most of Mark's former classmates headed to Chuck's farmhouse for lunch. Mark's mother and father were there, obviously waiting for me. "We want to show you something," his father said, taking a wallet out of his pocket. "They found this on Mark when he was killed. We thought you might recognize it."

Opening the billfold, he carefully removed two worn pieces of notebook paper that had obviously been taped, folded and refolded many times. I knew without looking that the papers were the ones on which I had listed all the good things each of Mark's classmates had said about him. "Thank you so much for doing that," Mark's mother said. "As you can see, Mark treasured it."

Mark's classmates started to gather around us. Chuck smiled rather sheepishly and said, "I still have my list. It's in the top drawer of my desk at home." John's wife said, "John asked me to put his in our wedding album." "I have mine too," Marilyn said. "It's in my diary." Then Vicki, another classmate, reached into her pocketbook, took out her wallet and showed her worn and frazzled list to the group. "I carry this with me at all times," Vicky said without batting an eyelash. "I think we all saved our lists."

That's when I finally sat down and cried.[3]

What would make so many adults hold on to pieces of paper they had received years before as kids, some of them carrying those pages with them everywhere they went—even into battle in a rice paddy halfway around the world? The answer is appreciation. Everyone is incredibly hungry for appreciation and recognition. As you interact with people, walk slowly through the crowd. Remember people's names and take time to show them you care. Make other people a priority in your life over every other thing, including your agenda and schedule. And give others recognition at every opportunity. It will build them up and motivate them. And it will make you a person of significant influence in their lives.

Encouragement

An experiment was conducted years ago to measure people's capacity to endure pain. Psychologists measured how long a barefooted person could stand in a bucket of ice water. They found that one factor made it possible for some people to stand in the ice water twice as long as others. Can you guess what that factor was? It was encouragement. When another person was present, giving support and encouragement, the sufferers were able to endure the pain much longer than their unencouraged counterparts.

When a person feels encouraged, he can face the impossible and overcome incredible adversity.

Few things help a person the way encouragement does. George M. Adams called it "oxygen to the soul." German philosopher-poet Johann Wolfgang von Goethe wrote, "Correction does much, but encouragement after censure is as the sun after a shower." And William A. Ward revealed his feelings when he said: "Flatter me, and I may not believe you. Criticize me, and I may not like you. Ignore me, and I may not forgive you. Encourage me, and I will not forget you."

The ability to influence is a natural by-product of encouragement. Benjamin Franklin wrote in a letter to naval commander John Paul Jones, "Hereafter, if you should observe an occasion to give your officers and friends a little more praise than is their due, and confess more fault than you can justly be charged with, you will only become the sooner for it, a great captain." Jones evidently learned the lesson. He eventually became a hero of the American Revolution and later achieved the rank of rear admiral in the Russian navy.

Just as encouragement makes others want to follow you, withholding praise and encouragement has the opposite effect. We read an account by Dr. Maxwell Maltz that shows the incredible negative impact a person can have when he doesn't encourage persons close to him. Maltz described a woman who came to his office seeking his help. Evidently, her son had moved from her home in the Midwest to New York where Maltz had his practice. When their son was only a boy, the woman's husband died, and she ran his business, hoping to do so only until the son became old enough to take it over. But when the son became old enough, he didn't want to be involved with it. Instead, he wanted to go to New York and study. She came to Maltz because she wanted him to find out why her son had behaved that way.

A few days later the son came to Maltz's office, explaining that his mother had insisted on the visit. "I love my mother," he explained, "but I've never told her why I had to leave home. I've just never had the courage. And I don't want her to be unhappy. But you see, Doctor, I don't want to take over what my father started. I want to make it on my own."

"That's very admirable," Maltz said to him, "but what do you have against your father?"

"My father was a good man and worked hard, but I suppose I resented him," he said. "My father came up the hard way. And he thought he should be tough on me. I guess he wanted to build self-reliance in me or something. When I was a boy, he never encouraged me. I can remember playing catch with him out in the yard. He'd pitch and I'd catch. We had a game to see if I could catch ten balls in a row. And, Doctor, he'd never let me catch the tenth ball! He'd throw eight or nine to me, but he always threw the tenth ball into the air, or into the ground, or where I couldn't catch it." The young man paused for a moment and then said, "He would never let me catch the tenth ball—never! And I guess I had to leave home and the business he started because I wanted somehow to catch that tenth ball!"

Lack of encouragement can hinder a person from living a healthy, productive life. But when a person feels encouraged, he can face the impossible and overcome incredible adversity. And the person who gives the gift of encouragement becomes an influencer in his life.

WHAT THEY RECEIVE

To become a nurturer, learn to be other-minded. Instead of thinking of yourself, put others first. Instead of putting others in their place, try to put *yourself* in their place. That's not always easy. Only when you have a sense of peace about yourself and who you are will you be able to be other-minded and give yourself away to others. But the rewards of nurturing are many. When you nurture people, they receive several things:

Positive Self-Worth

Nathaniel Branden, a psychiatrist and expert on the subject of self-esteem, states that no factor is more decisive in people's psychological development and motivation than the value judgments they make about themselves. He says that the nature of self-evaluation has a profound effect on a person's values, beliefs, thinking processes, feelings, needs, and goals. In his view, self-esteem is the most significant key to a person's behavior.

A poor self-concept can have all kinds of negative effects on a person's life. Poet T. S. Eliot asserted, "Half of the harm that is done in this world is due to people who want to feel important. . . . They do not mean to do harm. . . . They are absorbed in the endless struggle to think well of themselves." Poor self-worth creates an invisible ceiling that can stop a person from attempting to rise above self-imposed limitations.

If you are confident and have a healthy self-image, then you may be saying, "Hey, I can see trying to boost a child's self-worth, but when it comes to my employees or colleagues, let them take care of themselves. They're adults. They need to get over it." The reality is that most people, whether they're seven or fifty-seven, could use help with their feelings about themselves. They would love to have their sense of identity boosted. If you question that, try this experiment. Ask a couple of people you know to write down on a piece of paper all their personality strengths. Each person usually comes up with about half a dozen. Then ask them to write down all their weaknesses. Most of the time, the lists of weaknesses are at least twice as long!

Eighteenth-century writer-critic Samuel Johnson expressed this thought: "Self-confidence is the first great requisite to great undertakings." Self-esteem impacts every aspect of a person's life: employment, education, relationships, and more. For example, the National Institute for Student Motivation conducted a study showing that the impact of self-confidence on academic achievement is greater than that of IQ. And Martin Seligman, a professor of psychology at the University of Pennsylvania, discovered that people with high self-esteem get better-paying jobs and are more successful in their careers than people with low self-esteem. When he surveyed representatives of a major life insurance company, he found that those who expected to succeed sold 37 percent more insurance than those who did not.

If you want to help people improve their quality of life, become more productive at work, and develop more positive relationships, then build their self-worth. Make them feel good about themselves, and the positive benefits will spill over into every aspect of their lives. And when they begin to experience those benefits, they will be grateful to you.

Sense of Belonging

Belonging is one of the most basic human needs. When people feel isolated and excluded from a sense of communion with others, they suffer. Albert LaLonde pointed out the dangers of this isolation: "Many young people today have never experienced a deep emotional attachment to anyone. They do not know how to love and be loved. The need to be loved translates itself into the need to belong to someone or something. Driven by their need . . . they will do anything to belong."

Positive influencers understand this need for a sense of belonging and do things that make people feel included. Parents make sure their children feel like important members of the family. Spouses make the person to whom they are married feel like a cherished equal partner. And bosses let their employees know that they are valued members of the team.

Great leaders are particularly talented at making their followers feel they belong. Napoleon Bonaparte, for example, was a master at making people feel important and included. He was known for wandering through his camp and greeting every officer by name. As he talked to each man, he asked about his hometown, wife, and family. And the general talked about a battle or maneuver in which he knew the man had taken part. The interest and time he took with his followers made them feel a sense of camaraderie and belonging. It's no wonder that his men were devoted to him.

If you desire to become a better nurturer of people, develop an other-person mind-set. Look for ways to include others. Become like the farmer who used to hitch up his old mule to a two-horse plow every day and say, "Get up, Beauregard. Get up, Satchel. Get up, Robert. Get up, Betty Lou."

One day his neighbor, hearing the farmer, asked, "How many names does that mule have?"

"Oh, he has only one," answered the farmer. "His name is Pete. But I put blinders on him and call out all the other names so he will think other mules are working with him. He has a better attitude when he's a part of a team."

Perspective

Another thing that people gain when they are nurtured is a better perspective on themselves. Most people receive more than their share of negative comments and criticism from others—so much that they sometimes begin to lose sight of their value. There is a telling example of this in *A Touch of Wonder* by Arthur Gordon. He relates the story of a friend who belonged to a club at the University of Wisconsin. It was comprised of several bright young men who had genuine talent for writing. Each time they met, one of the men would read a story or essay he had written, and the rest of the group would dissect and criticize it. The viciousness of their comments prompted them to call themselves the Stranglers.

On the same campus, some women formed a group, and they called themselves the Wranglers. They also read their manuscripts to one another, but instead of showering criticism on one another, they tried to find positive things to say. Every member was given encouragement, no matter how weak or undeveloped her writing was.

For most people, it's not
what they are that holds them back.
It's what they think they're not.

The results of the two groups' activities came to light twenty years later when the careers of the classmates were examined. Of the talented young men in the Stranglers, not one of them had made a name for himself as a writer. But half a dozen successful writers emerged from the Wranglers, even though they had not necessarily shown greater promise. And some of the women had gained national prominence, such as Pulitzer prize–winner Marjorie Kinnan Rawlings.[4]

For most people, it's not what they are that holds them back. It's what they think they're not. The Stranglers undoubtedly made one another suspect that they were unqualified to write, and in time they became convinced of it. Who knows what kind of talent was squashed by their negativism? But if someone in the group had taken the initiative to be nurturing instead of negative, maybe another Hemingway, Faulkner, or Fitzgerald would have emerged and given the world another library of masterpieces.

Everyone appreciates being nurtured, even great men and women. A small exhibit at the Smithsonian Institution bears this out. It contains the personal effects found on Abraham Lincoln the night he was shot: a small handkerchief embroidered "A. Lincoln," a country boy's penknife, a spectacle case repaired with cotton string, a Confederate five-dollar bill, and a worn-out newspaper clipping extolling his accomplishments as president. It begins, "Abe Lincoln is one of the greatest statesmen of all time . . ."[5]

As we mentioned in the previous chapter, Lincoln faced fierce criticism while in office, and it would have been easy for him to become totally discouraged. That article, worn with repeated reading, undoubtedly helped him during some very difficult times. It nurtured him and helped him retain his perspective.

Feeling of Significance

Woody Allen once quipped, "My only regret in life is that I'm not someone else." And while he probably said that to get a laugh, with the relationship problems he has had over the years, we can't help wondering how much truth there is to his comment. In life, the price tag that the world puts on us is almost identical to the one we put on ourselves. People who have a great deal of self-respect and who believe that they have significance are usually respected and made to feel valued by others.

When you nurture people and add value to them without expecting anything in return, they feel significant. They realize that they are valued, that they matter to others. And once they consistently feel positive about themselves, they're free to live more positively for themselves and others.

Hope

Writer Mark Twain warned, "Keep away from people who try to belittle your ambitions. Small people always do that, but the really great make you feel that you, too, can become great." How do most people feel when they're around you? Do they feel small and insignificant, or do they believe in themselves and have hope about what they can become?

The key to how you *treat* people lies in how you *think* about them. It's a matter of attitude. How you act reveals what you believe. Johann Wolfgang von Goethe emphasized, "Treat a man as he appears to be and you make him worse. But treat a man as if he already were what he potentially could be, and you make him what he should be."

Hope is perhaps the greatest gift you can give others as the result of nurturing, because even if their sense of self is weak and they fail to see their own significance, they still have a reason to keep trying and striving to reach their potential in the future.

In *Building Your Mate's Self-Esteem,* Dennis Rainey tells a wonderful story about nurturing hope that can lead to the development of tremendous potential. He says that there was a boy named Tommy who had a particularly hard time in school. He continually asked questions, and he never could quite keep up. It seemed that he failed every time he tried something. His teacher finally gave up on him and told his mother that he could not learn and would never amount to much. But Tommy's mother was a nurturer. She believed in him. She taught him at home, and each time he failed, she gave him hope and encouraged him to keep trying.

What ever happened to Tommy? He became an inventor, eventually holding more than one thousand patents, including those of the phonograph and the first commercially practical incandescent electric lightbulb. His name was Thomas Edison.[6] When people have hope, there is no telling how far they can go.

How to Become a Natural Nurturer

Maybe you weren't born a nurturing person. Many people find it hard to be loving and positive to others, especially if the environment they grew up in wasn't particularly uplifting. But anyone can become a nurturer and add value to others. If you cultivate a positive attitude of other-mindedness, you, too, can become a natural at nurturing and enjoy the added privilege of influence in the lives of others. Here's how to do it:

- **Commit to them.** Make a commitment to become a nurturer. Making a commitment to help people changes your priorities and your actions. Love for others always finds a way to help; indifference to others finds nothing but excuses.
- **Believe in them.** People rise or fall to meet the expectations of those closest to them. Give people your trust and hope, and they will do everything they can to keep from letting you down.
- **Be accessible to them.** You can't nurture anyone from a distance. You can only do it up close. When you first start the process with people, you may need to spend a lot of time with them. But as they

gain confidence in themselves and the relationship, they will require less personal contact. Until they reach that point, make sure they have access to you.

- **Give with no strings attached.** If you need people, you cannot lead them. And nurturing is an aspect of leadership. Instead of trying to make a transaction out of it, give freely without expecting anything in return. Nineteenth-century economist Henry Drummond wisely observed, "You will find as you look back upon your life that the moments when you have really lived are the moments when you have done things in a spirit of love."

- **Give them opportunities.** As the people you nurture gain strength, give them additional opportunities to succeed and grow. You will continue to nurture them, but as time goes by, their actions and accomplishments will help them remain secure, respected, and encouraged.

- **Lift them to a higher level.** Your ultimate goal should always be to help people go to a higher level, to reach their potential. Nurturing is the foundation upon which they can begin the building process.

Walt Disney is reported to have said that there are three kinds of people in the world. There are well-poisoners who discourage others, stomp on their creativity, and tell them what they can't do. There are lawn-mowers, people who have good intentions but are self-absorbed, who mow their own lawns but never help others. And there are life-enhancers. This last category contains people who reach out to enrich the lives of others, who lift them up and inspire them. Each of us needs to do everything in our power to become a life-enhancer, to nurture people so that they are motivated to grow and reach their potential. It is a process that takes time. (And in coming chapters, we'll share insights that will show you how to help people take additional steps in that process.)

One of the most inspiring stories of encouragement and nurturing we've ever heard concerns John Wesley—an influencer we mentioned in this book's introduction. In 1791, Wesley wrote a letter to William Wilberforce, a member of England's Parliament who was in the midst of fighting for the abolition of the British slave trade. The letter, which has since become famous, said this:

London, February 26, 1791
Dear Sir:

Unless the divine power has raised you up . . . I see not how you can go through your glorious enterprise, in opposing that execrable villainy, which is the scandal of religion, of England, and of human nature. Unless God has raised you up for this very thing, you will be worn out by the opposition of men and devils. But "if God be for you, who can be against you?" Are all of them stronger than God? O "be not weary in well doing!" Go on, in the name of God and in the power of His might, till even American slavery (the vilest that ever saw the sun) shall vanish away before it . . .

That He who has guided you from your youth up, may continue to strengthen you in this and all things, is the prayer of,

Your affectionate servant,
J. Wesley

Four days later, Wesley was dead at age eighty-eight, yet his influence in Wilberforce's life continued for years. Wilberforce did not succeed in convincing Parliament to abolish slavery at that time, but he didn't give up the fight. He kept at it for decades despite slander, vilification, and threats. And when he thought he couldn't go on, he looked to Wesley's letter for encouragement. Finally, in 1807, the slave trade was abolished. And in 1833, several months after Wilberforce's death, slavery was outlawed in all of the British Empire.

Though condemned by many during his career, Wilberforce was buried with honor in Westminster Abbey, one of the most esteemed men of his day. Part of his epitaph reads:

Eminent as he was in every department of public labour,
  And a leader in every work of charity,
Whether to relieve the temporal or the spiritual wants
  of his fellow men
His name will ever be specially identified
  With those exertions
Which, by the blessing of God, removed from England
  The guilt of the African slave trade,
And prepared the way for the abolition of slavery
  in every colony of the Empire.

Maybe there is a William Wilberforce in your life, just waiting to be nurtured to greatness. The only way you'll ever know is to become a nurturer who is other-minded and adds value to the people you meet.

<u>Influence Checklist</u>
NURTURING OTHER PEOPLE

❑ **Develop a nurturing environment in your home, place of business, or church.** Make it your goal to make the people around you feel loved, respected, and secure. To do that, commit to eliminating all negative criticism from your speech for one month and searching for only positive things to say to others.

❑ **Give special encouragement.** Pick two or three people to encourage this month. Send each person a short handwritten note every week. Make yourself accessible to these people. And give of your time without expecting something in return. At the end of the month, examine your relationships with them for positive change.

❑ **Rebuild bridges.** Think of one person with whom you have tended to be negative in the past. (It can be anyone: a colleague, a family member, or an employee, for instance.) Go to that person and apologize for your past actions or remarks. Then find the quality you most admire about the person and tell him or her about it. During the following weeks, look for ways to build and strengthen the relationship.

CHAPTER 3

A Person of Influence Has . . .

FAITH IN PEOPLE

MULTIPLY

MENTOR

MOTIVATE—*Faith*

MODEL

Jim grew up in Niagara Falls, New York. Today the population is about 60,000, but when Jim lived there, it had closer to 100,000 people. It was a thriving industrial center, with companies such as DuPont Chemical. It also had cultural offerings, a strong one-hundred-year-old university, and other attractions, but the main focus of the town then was the incredible natural wonder of the falls, as it still is today.

The Iroquois called it *Niagara,* meaning "thunder of waters." It's an awesome sight. Every minute more than 12 million cubic feet of water drop a distance of about 180 feet over the edge of the falls. And its total width, including both the Canadian and the American portions, measures more than 3,100 feet. It is rightly called one of the natural wonders of the world. Jim says:

Back when we were growing up, we heard a lot of stories about the falls and the daredevil stunts people used to pull—like Annie Edson Taylor's going over the falls in a barrel and things like that. One of the great legends of the town was a French acrobat named Charles Blondin who lived from 1824 to 1897. He crossed over the entire width of the falls on a tightrope back in 1859. That must have taken nerves of steel since a fall certainly would have killed him. In fact, he crossed the falls several times. He did it once with a wheelbarrow, another time blind-folded, and yet another time on stilts. They say he was quite remarkable. He continued performing even into his seventies.

One of the most incredible feats he performed was crossing the falls on a tightrope while carrying a man on his back. Can you imagine that? I guess just crossing over by himself wasn't tough enough for him! But as difficult as that feat must have been on Blondin, I can't help wondering how he got someone to go with him. That's what you call trust: to climb onto the back of a man who is going to walk more than half a mile on *a rope* suspended over one of the most powerful waterfalls in the world.

I used to think about that as a kid. What would it be like to see the falls from up on a rope above them? And more importantly, what person would trust me to carry him across the falls the way that man trusted Blondin?

FACTS ABOUT FAITH IN PEOPLE

We can't tell you the identity of the man Blondin carried across the falls, but there is no question that he had great faith in the French acrobat. After all, he put his life in the man's hands. You don't see that kind of trust in others every day. But the times you do, it is a very special thing.

Faith in people is an essential quality of an influencer when working with others, yet it's a scarce commodity today. Take a look at the following four facts about faith:

1. Most People Don't Have Faith in Themselves

Not long ago we saw a *Shoe* comic strip by Jeff MacNelly that showed Shoe, the crusty newspaper editor, standing on the mound in a baseball game. His catcher said to him, "You've got to have faith in your curve ball." In the next frame Shoe remarked, "It's easy for him to say. When it comes to believing in myself, I'm an agnostic."

> *When you believe in people,*
> *they do the impossible.*
> —Nancy Dornan

That's the way too many people feel today. They have trouble believing in themselves. They believe they will fail. Even when they see a light at the end of the tunnel, they're convinced it's a train. They see a difficulty in every possibility. But the reality is that difficulties seldom defeat people; lack of faith in themselves usually does it. With a little faith in themselves, people can do miraculous things. But without it, they have a really tough time.

2.   Most People Don't Have Someone Who Has Faith in Them

In *Just for Today,* James Keller tells this story: "A sidewalk flower vendor was not doing any business. Suddenly a happy thought struck him and he put up this sign: 'This gardenia will make you feel important all day long for 10 cents.' All at once his sales began to increase."

In our society today, most people feel isolated. The strong sense of community that was once enjoyed by most Americans has become rare. And many people don't have the family support that was more common thirty or forty years ago. For example, evangelist Bill Glass noted, "Over 90 percent of prison inmates were told by parents while growing up, 'They're going to put you in jail.'" Instead of teaching their children to believe in themselves, some parents are tearing them down. For many people, even those who are closest to them don't believe in them. They have no one on their side. No wonder even a little thing like a flower can make a difference in how a person approaches the day.

3.   Most People Can Tell When Someone Has Faith in Them

People's instincts are pretty good at knowing when others have faith in them. They can sense if your belief is genuine or phony. And truly having faith in someone can change her life. Jim's wife, Nancy, often says, "When you believe in people, they do the impossible."

In his book *Move Ahead with Possibility Thinking,* John's friend Robert Schuller, pastor of the Crystal Cathedral in Garden Grove, California, tells a wonderful story about an incident that changed his life as a boy. It occurred when his uncle had faith in him and showed it in his words and actions:

His car drove past the unpainted barn and stopped in a cloud of summer dust at our front gate. I ran barefooted across the splintery porch and saw my uncle Henry bound out of the car. He was tall, very handsome, and terribly alive with energy. After many years overseas as a missionary in China, he was visiting our Iowa farm. He ran up to the old gate and put both of his big hands on my four-year-old shoulders.

He smiled widely, ruffled my uncombed hair, and said, "Well! I guess you're Robert! I think you are going to be a preacher someday." That night I prayed secretly, "And dear God, make me a preacher when I grow up!" I believe that God made me a POSSIBILITY THINKER then and there.

As you work to become a person of influence, always remember that your goal is not to get people to think more highly of you. It's to get them to think more highly of themselves. Have faith in them, and they will begin to do exactly that.

Difficulties seldom defeat people; lack of faith in themselves usually does it.

4.   Most People Will Do Anything to Live Up to Your Faith in Them

People rise or fall to meet your level of expectations for them. If you express skepticism and doubt in others, they will return your lack of confidence with mediocrity. But if you believe in them and expect them to do well, they will go the extra mile trying to do their best. And in the process, they and you benefit. John H. Spalding expressed the thought this way: "Those who believe in our ability do more than stimulate us. They create for us an atmosphere in which it becomes easier to succeed."

If you've never been one to trust people and put your faith in them, change your way of thinking and begin believing in others. Your life will quickly improve. When you have faith in others, you give them an incredible gift. Give others money, and it's soon spent. Give resources, and they may not be used to their best advantage. Give help, and people will often find themselves back where they started in a short period of time. But give them your faith, and they become confident, energized, and self-reliant. They become motivated to acquire what they need to succeed on their own. And then later if you share money, resources, and help, they're better able to use them to build a better future.

FAITH IS BELIEF IN ACTION

In the late 1800s, a salesman from back east arrived at a frontier town somewhere on the Great Plains. As he was talking to the owner of a general store, a rancher came in, and the owner excused himself to take care of his customer. As they talked, the salesman couldn't help overhearing their conversation. It seemed the rancher wanted credit for some things he needed.

"Are you doing any fencing this spring, Jake?" asked the storekeeper.

"Sure am, Bill," said the rancher.

"Fencing in or fencing out?"

"Fencing in. Taking in another 360 acres across the creek."

"Good to hear it, Jake. You got the credit. Just tell Steve out back what you need."

The salesman was dumbfounded. "I've seen all kinds of credit systems," he said, "but never one like that. How does it work?"

"Well," said the storekeeper, "let me tell you. If a man's fencing out, that means he's scared, trying to just hold on to what he's got. But if he's fencing in, he's growing and trying to improve. I always give credit to a man who's fencing in because that means he believes in himself."

Having faith in people requires more than just words or positive feelings about them. We have to back it up with what we do. As W. T. Purkiser, professor emeritus of religion at Point Loma College, clearly saw: "Faith is more than thinking something is true. Faith is thinking something is true to the extent that we act on it."

If you want to help other people and make a positive impact on their lives, you have to treat them with that kind of confidence. Ralph Waldo Emerson said, "Trust men and they will be true to you; treat them greatly and they will show themselves great." Become a believer in people, and even the most tentative and inexperienced people can bloom right before your eyes.

How to Become a
Believer in People

We're fortunate because we grew up in positive, affirming environments. As a result, we have an easy time believing in people and expressing that belief. But we realize that not everyone had the benefit of a positive upbringing. Most people need to *learn* how to have faith in others. To build your belief in others, try using these suggestions, created using the initial letters of the word *BELIEVE.*

Believe in Them Before They Succeed

Have you ever noticed how many people support a sports team as soon as it starts winning? That happened here in San Diego a couple of years ago when the Chargers won their division, then won all their play-off games leading into the Super Bowl. The whole town went crazy. You could see the team's lightning bolt symbol everywhere: on people's houses, on the back windows of cars, on lapel pins, and so forth.

During the height of the Chargers' success, a couple of local radio personalities named Jeff and Jer rallied the people of San Diego by sponsoring a big event at the stadium one morning. Their plan was to give the people who showed up T-shirts in the team colors and have them line up in the parking lot in the shape of a giant lightning bolt. Then they would take a picture of it from a helicopter and put it in the newspaper the next morning. A couple of thousand people were required to pull it off, but they hoped enough would show to make it happen. Imagine their surprise when so many people showed up that they ran out of T-shirts, and ended up surrounding the "human bolt" with a border of extras. It was such a big deal that some of the news services picked it up and televised it on the national news.

Everyone loves a winner. It's easy to have faith in people who have already proved themselves. It's much tougher to believe in people *before* they have proved themselves. But that is the key to motivating people to reach their potential. You have to believe in them first, before they become successful, and sometimes before they even believe in themselves. French writer and moralist Joseph Joubert said, "No one can give faith unless he has faith. It is the persuaded who persuade." You need faith in others before you can persuade them to believe in themselves.

Some people in your life desperately want to believe in themselves but have little hope. As you interact with them, remember the motto of French World War I hero Marshal Ferdinand Foch: "There are no hopeless situations; there are only men and women who have grown hopeless about them." Every person has seeds of greatness within, even though they may currently be dormant. But when you believe in people, you water the seeds and give them the chance to grow. Every time you put your faith in them, you're giving life-sustaining water, warmth, food, and light. And if you continue to give encouragement through your belief in them, these people will bloom in time.

Emphasize Their Strengths

We mentioned previously that many people mistakenly think that to be influential in other people's lives, they have to be an "authority" and point out others' deficiencies. People who try that approach become like Lucy from the comic strip *Peanuts* by Charles Schulz. In one strip Lucy told poor Charlie Brown, "You, Charlie Brown, are a foul ball in the line drive of life! You're in the shadow of your own goal posts! You are a miscue! You are three putts on the eighteenth green! You are a seven-ten split in the tenth frame. . . . You are a missed free throw, a shanked nine iron and a called third strike! Do you understand? Have I made myself clear?" That's hardly a way to positively impact the life of another person!

The road to becoming a positive influence on others lies in exactly the opposite direction. The best way to show people your faith in them and motivate them is to focus your attention on their strengths. According to author and advertising executive Bruce Barton, "Nothing splendid has ever been achieved except by those who dared believe that something inside them was superior to circumstances." By emphasizing people's strengths, you're helping them believe that they possess what they need to succeed.

*Believing in people before they have proved
themselves is the key to motivating people
to reach their potential.*

Praise them for what they do well, both privately and publicly. Tell
them how much you appreciate their positive qualities and their skills.
And anytime you have the opportunity to compliment and praise them
in the presence of their family and close friends, do it.

List Their Past Successes

Even when you emphasize people's strengths, they may need further
encouragement to show them you believe in them and to get them motivated. Entrepreneur Mary Kay Ash advised, "Everyone has an invisible
sign hanging from his neck saying, 'Make me feel important!' Never forget this message when working with people." One of the best ways to do
that is to help people remember their past successes.

The account of David and Goliath presents a classic example of how
past successes can help a person have faith in himself. You may remember the story from the Bible. A nine-foot-tall Philistine champion
named Goliath stood before the army of Israel and taunted them every
day for forty days, daring them to send out a warrior to face him. On
the fortieth day a young shepherd named David came to the front lines
to deliver food to his brothers, who were in Israel's army. While he was
there, he witnessed the giant's contemptuous display of taunts and challenges. David was so infuriated that he told King Saul of Israel that he
wanted to face the giant in battle. Here's what happened:

David said to Saul, "Let no one lose heart on account of this Philistine;
your servant will go and fight him." Saul replied, "You are not able to
go out against this Philistine and fight him; you are only a boy, and he
has been a fighting man from his youth." But David said to Saul, "Your

servant has been keeping his father's sheep. When a lion or a bear came and carried off a sheep from the flock, I went after it, struck it and rescued the sheep from its mouth. When it turned on me, I seized it by its hair, struck it and killed it. Your servant has killed both the lion and the bear. . . . The LORD who delivered me from the paw of the lion and the paw of the bear will deliver me from the hand of this Philistine."[1]

David looked back on his past successes, and he had confidence in his future actions. And of course, when he faced the giant, he felled him like a tree, using nothing but a rock and sling. And when he cut off Goliath's head, his success inspired his fellow countrymen; they routed the Philistine army.

Not everyone has the natural ability to recognize past successes and draw confidence from them. Some people need help. If you can show others that they have done well in the past and help them see that their past victories have paved the way for future success, they'll be better able to move into action. Listing past successes helps others believe in themselves.

Instill Confidence When They Fail

When you have encouraged people and put your faith in them, and they begin to believe they can succeed in life, they soon reach a critical crossroads. The first time or two that they fail—and they will fail because it's a part of life—they have two choices. They can give in or go on.

Some people are resilient and willing to keep trying in order to succeed, even when they don't see immediate progress. But others aren't that determined. Some will collapse at the first sign of trouble. To give them a push and inspire them, you need to keep showing your confidence in them, even when they're making mistakes or doing poorly.

One of the ways to do that is to tell them about your past troubles and traumas. Sometimes people think that if you're currently successful, you have always been that way. They don't realize that you have had your share of flops, failures, and fumbles. Show them that success is a journey, a process, not a destination. When they realize that you have failed and yet still managed to succeed, they'll realize that it's okay to fail. And their confidence will remain intact. They will learn to think the way baseball legend Babe Ruth did when he said, "Never let the fear of striking out get in the way."

Experience Some Wins Together

It's not enough just knowing that failure is a part of moving forward in life. To really become motivated to succeed, people need to believe they can win. John, like many of us, got a taste for winning when he was just a kid. He says,

> Growing up, I idolized my brother Larry, who is two and a half years older than I am. After my parents, he was probably the greatest influencer in my life when I was a kid. Larry has always been a great leader and an excellent athlete. And whenever we played basketball, football, or baseball with the kids in the neighborhood, Larry was a captain.
>
> A lot of times when they picked teams, I would be one of the last picked, because I was younger and smaller than most of the kids. But as I got older, Larry began picking me more, and that always made me feel good, not only because it meant my brother cared about me, but because I knew that when Larry picked me, I was going to be on the winning team. You see, Larry was a fierce competitor, and he didn't like losing. He always played to win, and he usually did. Together we put quite a few wins under our belts, and I came to expect victory when I played with my brother.

Winning is motivating. Novelist David Ambrose acknowledged this truth: "If you have the will to win, you have achieved half your success; if you don't, you have achieved half your failure." Coming alongside others to help them experience some wins with you gives them reasons to believe they will succeed. And in the process, they sense victory. That's when incredible things begin to happen in their lives. Take a look at this comparison between what happens when people sense victory versus when they expect defeat:

When People Sense Victory	When People Sense Defeat
they sacrifice to succeed.	they give as little as possible.
they look for ways to win.	they look for excuses.
they become energized.	they become tired.
they follow the game plan.	they forsake the game plan.
they help other team members.	they hurt others.

To help people believe they can achieve victory, put them in a position to experience small successes. Encourage them to perform tasks or take on responsibilities you know they can handle and do well. And give them the assistance they need to succeed. As Greek orator Demosthenes said, "Small opportunities are often the beginning of great enterprises." In time as their confidence grows, they will take on more difficult challenges, but they will be able to face them with confidence and competence because of the positive track record they're developing.

Visualize Their Future Success

We heard about an experiment performed with laboratory rats to measure their motivation to live under different circumstances. Scientists dropped a rat into a jar of water that had been placed in total darkness, and they timed how long the animal would continue swimming before it gave up and allowed itself to drown. They found that the rat usually lasted little more than three minutes.

Then they dropped another rat into the same kind of jar, but instead of placing it in total darkness, they allowed a ray of light to shine into it. Under those circumstances, the rat kept swimming for thirty-six hours. That's more than seven hundred times longer than the one in the dark! Because the rat could see, it continued to have hope.

If that is true of laboratory animals, think of how strong the effect of visualization can be on people, who are capable of higher reasoning. It's been said that a person can live forty days without food, four days without water, four minutes without air, but only four seconds without hope. Each time you cast a vision for others and paint a picture of their future success, you build them up, motivate them, and give them reasons to keep going.

Expect a New Level of Living

German statesman Konrad Adenauer observed: "We all live under the same sky, but we don't all have the same horizon." As an influencer, you have the goal of helping others see beyond today and their current circumstances and dream big dreams. When you put your faith in people, you help them to expand their horizons and motivate them to move to a whole new level of living.

> *To help people believe they can achieve*
> *victory, put them in a position to*
> *experience small successes.*

Integral to that new way of living is a change in attitude. According to Denis Waitley, "The winner's edge is not in a gifted birth, a high IQ, or in talent. The winner's edge is all in the attitude, not aptitude. Attitude is the criterion for success." As people's attitudes change from doubt to confidence—in themselves and their ability to succeed and reach their potential—everything in their lives changes for the better.

Jim and Nancy gained incredible insights about the power of putting their faith into others several years ago when they decided to take a chance with their son Eric on a mountain in Utah. Here's Jim's account of it:

When you have a disabled child, you constantly fight a battle of emotions between providing him new experiences and protecting him from injury or failure. Our life with Eric has been no exception. Despite his limitations, which include having to use a wheelchair and having very little use in his right hand, Eric has a great positive spirit. Often if there is hesitation to try new things, it comes from Nancy and me rather than him.

About five years ago Nancy got the idea that we should take Eric skiing. She had heard from a friend about a place in Park City, Utah, called the National Ability Center. There they offer people with disabilities instruction and assistance in snow skiing, swimming, tennis, waterskiing, horseback riding, rafting, and other activities. She thought the experience would be great for his self-esteem.

I have to admit, I was skeptical about it from the very beginning. Knowing how difficult the sport is for me, I had trouble imagining Eric racing down a 10,000-foot mountain. And that wasn't helped by the knowledge that a blow to Eric's head could cause him to have a seizure that would put him in the hospital for more brain surgery. But Nancy had faith that Eric could do it, and when she believes, so does he. And off we went to give it a try.

When we got up to Deer Valley and met some of the people who work at the National Ability Center, I started to feel a little bit better about it. They were professional and extremely positive, and they showed us the equipment that Eric would be using, a type of bi-ski with a molded seat. Eric would be put in the chair and steer using a bar attached to outrigger skis.

When we started to fill out paperwork, we were momentarily paralyzed when we read the waiver that said that Eric would be "engaging in activities that involve risk of serious injury, including permanent disability and death." It made the risk seem very real, but by this time Eric was very excited and we didn't want him to see any hesitation from us.

After Velcro-fastening Eric into his bi-ski and giving him some pointers, Stephanie, his young instructor, took him up the bunny slope. About ten minutes later, we got excited as we saw Eric coming down the hill with the biggest smile on his face. We were so proud of him that we were giving him high fives and patting him on the back. I thought to myself, *That wasn't so bad.*

Then off they went again. What we didn't know was that this time they were going to the top of the mountain. At the bottom of the hill we waited. And waited. We weren't sure whether we'd see Eric come down the mountain on his skis or on a stretcher with the ski patrol. Finally after about thirty minutes, we saw him and Stephanie come around a bend and ski to the bottom of the slope. His cheeks were flushed, and he was grinning like the Cheshire cat. He loved it.

"Move over, Dad," he said as he blew past us. "I'm going up again."

Eric skied every day on that trip. In fact, when he finished skiing one day, he told us, "Stephanie didn't take me up the mountain today."

"Oh," said Nancy, "then who skied with you?"

"Some one-legged guy," answered Eric.

"What!" screeched Nancy. "What do you mean some one-legged guy?"

"Yep," said Eric, "a one-legged guy." And then Eric smiled mischievously and said, "Want to know how he lost his leg? Avalanche!"

Eric has been skiing every year since then, and his life hasn't been the same. He now has confidence that he never had before, and he is willing to try just about anything. He swims three days a week, works out with weights, plays power soccer, and does other sorts of things. I guess you could say that he has adopted the motto of the National Ability Center as his own: "If I Can Do This, I Can Do Anything!"

If they had done things Jim's way, Eric never would have gotten the chance to experience what he did on that mountain in Utah five years ago. Jim loves Eric with all his heart, but he tends to want to play it safe. Putting your faith in others involves taking a chance. But the rewards outweigh the risks. Robert Louis Stevenson said, "To be what we are, and to become what we are capable of becoming, is the only end of life." When you put your faith in others, you help them reach their potential. And you become an important influencer in their lives.

Influence Checklist
HAVING FAITH IN PEOPLE

❑ **Find a strength.** Think about someone you'd like to encourage. Find a strength that the person has, and point it out to him or her. Use your interaction as an opportunity to express confidence in the person.

❑ **Build on past successes.** If you have to give someone a difficult assignment in the near future, take some time to recall his or her past successes. Then when you meet with the person, review those past successes. (If you go through this process and can't recall any past successes, that's a sign you've spent too little time getting to know the person. Plan to spend some time together to get better acquainted.)

❑ **Help others overcome defeat.** If you have colleagues, friends, employees, or family members who have recently experienced a defeat of some kind, take time to chat with them about it. Let them tell you the whole story, and when they're done, make it clear that you value them and still believe strongly in them.

❑ **Start off right.** The next time you recruit new people for your organization, start the relationships right. Instead of waiting until after they prove themselves to praise them, make it a point to repeatedly express your faith in them and their ability *before* they give you results. You'll be pleased by their desire to live up to your positive expectations.

CHAPTER 4

A Person of Influence . . .

LISTENS
TO PEOPLE

MULTIPLY

MENTOR

MOTIVATE—*Listen*

MODEL

If you were going on a job interview today, what would you say is the most important skill you would need? Is it writing, to create a knockout résumé? Or maybe salesmanship? After all, isn't that what you do on an interview, sell yourself? Or how about charisma? If you're charismatic, you're sure to get the job you want, right?

Or let's say that instead of going on an interview, you were going to spend your day recruiting, whether for business prospects, ministry workers, or people to play on your softball team. What skill would you need as a recruiter? Discernment? An eye for talent? The ability to cast vision and get people excited? Or maybe it would be hard-nosed negotiation skills?

Better yet, let's say your job today was to supply new ideas for your organization. What qualities would you need? Creativity? Intelligence? Would you need a good education? What is the number one ability you would need?

No matter which one of these three tasks you were to take on today, you would need one skill over all others, more than talent, discernment, or charm. It is the one skill that all great leaders recognize as indispensable to their ability to influence others and succeed. Have you guessed what it is? It's the ability to listen.

Not everyone is quick to learn the lesson of the importance of listening. Take, for example, Jim's experience:

> Fresh from Purdue University's engineering school, I started out in the corporate environment at McDonnell-Douglas where they had about 40,000 employees. I was working in the advanced design group for the DC-10 doing wind-tunnel analyses and computer simulations of the airplane's performance.
>
> But it didn't take me long to realize that I wasn't going to be there for my whole career. Some of the guys I worked with had been there two decades, and nothing had changed in them for those twenty years. They were in a holding pattern, waiting for the gold watch. But I wanted to make a greater impact on my world.
>
> That's when I started to pursue other business opportunities, and

when I found the right one, I began trying to recruit others to join me. Back then my strategy was to meet people in the huge employee cafeteria. After waiting in line to get my lunch, I'd look for a seat next to a sharp-looking guy who was sitting by himself, and I'd strike up a conversation with him. The first chance I got, I'd bombard him with information and try to persuade him with impressive facts and irrefutable logic. I managed to intimidate a few people with the force of my convictions, but I was unsuccessful in building a productive relationship with anyone.

I'd been doing this for several months, with very little success, when one day I was just talking with a guy from another department. He was telling me about the frustrations he was having with his boss, and about some problems he was having at home. He just found out his oldest child needed braces, their old clunker of a car was on its last legs, and he wasn't sure how he was going to make it. I really felt for the guy, and I wanted to get to know him better. Then suddenly, I realized that I could help him out. He was feeling powerless on the job, and he had money problems—two things that could be helped by being in business for himself. So I started to tell him about my business and explain how it might solve some of his problems. And to my shock he was actually very interested.

That day it hit me: *What an idiot I've been! I can't succeed with others by dumping information on them. If I want to help them or have a positive impact on people, I need to learn how to listen to them!*

THE VALUE OF LISTENING

Edgar Watson Howe once joked, "No man would listen to you talk if he didn't know it was his turn next." Unfortunately, that accurately describes the way too many people approach communication—they're too busy waiting for their turn to really listen to others. But people of influence understand the incredible value of becoming a good listener. For example, when Lyndon B. Johnson was a junior senator from Texas, he kept a sign on his office wall that read, "You ain't learnin' nothin' when you're doin' all the talkin'." And Woodrow Wilson, the twenty-eighth American president, once said, "The ear of the leader must ring with the voices of the people."

The ability to skillfully listen is one key to gaining influence with others. Consider these benefits to listening that we've found:

Listening Shows Respect

Psychologist Dr. Joyce Brothers said, "Listening, not imitation, may be the sincerest form of flattery." Whenever you don't pay attention to what others have to say, you send them the message that you don't value them. But when you listen to others, you communicate that you respect them. Even more, you show them that you care. German-born philosopher-theologian Paul Tillich commented, "The first duty of love is to listen."

A mistake that people often make in communicating is trying very hard to impress the other person. They try to make themselves appear smart, witty, or entertaining. But if you want to relate well to others, you have to be willing to focus on what they have to offer. Be *impressed and interested*, not *impressive and interesting*. Poet-philosopher Ralph Waldo Emerson acknowledged, "Every man I meet is in some way my superior, and I can learn of him." Remember that and listen, and the lines of communication will really open up.

Listening Builds Relationships

Dale Carnegie, author of *How to Win Friends and Influence People*, advised, "You can make more friends in two weeks by becoming a good listener than you can in two years trying to get other people interested in you." Carnegie was incredibly gifted at understanding relationships. He recognized that people who are self-focused and who talk about themselves and their concerns all the time rarely develop strong relationships with others. David Schwartz noted in *The Magic of Thinking Big*, "Big people monopolize the listening. Small people monopolize the talking."

By becoming a good listener, you are able to connect with others on more levels and develop stronger, deeper relationships because you are meeting a need. Author C. Neil Strait pointed out that "everyone needs someone who he feels really listens to him." When you become that important listener, you help that person. And you take a significant step toward becoming a person of influence in his or her life.

Listening Increases Knowledge

Wilson Mizner said, "A good listener is not only popular everywhere, but after a while he knows something." It's amazing how much you can learn about your friends and family, your job, the organization you work in, and yourself when you decide to really listen to others. But not everyone clues in to this benefit. For example, we heard a story about a tennis pro who was giving a lesson to a new student. After watching the novice take several swings at the tennis ball, the pro stopped him and suggested ways he could improve his stroke. But each time he did, the student interrupted him and gave his opinion of the problem and how it should be solved. After several interruptions, the pro began to nod his head in agreement.

When the lesson ended, a woman who had been watching said to the pro, "Why did you go along with that arrogant man's stupid suggestions?"

> *You'll never know how close you are
> to a million-dollar idea unless
> you're willing to listen.*

The pro smiled and replied, "I learned a long time ago that it is a waste of time to try to sell real *answers* to anyone who just wants to buy *echoes*."

Beware of putting yourself into a position where you think you know all the answers. Anytime you do, you'll be putting yourself in danger. It's almost impossible to think of yourself as "the expert" and continue growing and learning at the same time. All great learners are great listeners.

One common problem as people gain more authority is that they often listen to others less and less, especially the people who report to them.

While it's true that the higher you go, the less you are required to listen to others, it's also true that your need for good listening skills increases. The farther you get from the front lines, the more you have to depend on others to get reliable information. Only if you develop good listening skills early, and then continue to use them, will you be able to gather the information you need to succeed.

As you proceed through life and become more successful, don't lose sight of your need to keep growing and improving yourself. And remember, a deaf ear is evidence of a closed mind.

Listening Generates Ideas

Fresh, innovative ideas help us to find new ways to solve old problems, to generate new products and processes to keep our organizations growing, and to continue growing and improving personally. Plutarch of ancient Greece asserted, "Know how to listen, and you will profit even from those who talk badly."

When we think about innovative companies that never seem to run out of ideas, 3M immediately comes to mind. That company seems to develop new products faster than just about any other manufacturer. The organization has a reputation for being open to employees' ideas and for listening to customers. In fact, a representative of 3M said the number one resource for product ideas was customer complaints.

Good companies have a reputation for listening to their people. Chili's restaurants, one of the nation's best-run food service chains according to *Restaurants and Institutions* magazine, is known for that quality too. Almost 80 percent of its menu has come from suggestions made by unit managers.

What's good for effective companies is good for individuals. When you consistently listen to others, you never suffer for ideas. People love to contribute, especially when their leader shares the credit with them. If you give people opportunities to share their thoughts, and you listen with an open mind, there will always be a flow of new ideas. And even if you hear ideas that won't work, just listening to them can often spark other creative thoughts in you and others. You'll never know how close you are to a million-dollar idea unless you're willing to listen.

Listening Builds Loyalty

A funny thing happens when you don't make a practice of listening to people. They find others who will. Anytime employees, spouses, colleagues, children, or friends no longer believe they are being listened to, they seek out people who will give them what they want. Sometimes the consequences can be disastrous: the end of a friendship, lack of authority at work, lessened parental influence, or the breakdown of a marriage.

> *Nobody ever listened himself*
> *or herself out of a sale.*

On the other hand, practicing good listening skills draws people to you. Karl Menninger, psychiatrist, author, and one of the founders of the Menninger Foundation, said, "The friends who listen to us are the ones we move toward, and we want to sit in their radius." Everyone loves a good listener and is attracted to him or her. And if you consistently listen to others, valuing them and what they have to offer, they are likely to develop a strong loyalty to you, even when your authority with them is unofficial or informal.

Listening Is a Great Way to Help Others and Yourself

Roger G. Imhoff urged, "Let others confide in you. It may not help you, but it surely will help them." At first glance, listening to others may appear to benefit only them. But when you become a good listener, you put yourself in a position to help yourself too. You have the ability to develop strong relationships, gather valuable information, and increase your understanding of yourself and others.

COMMON BARRIERS TO LISTENING

Few people have reached their potential when it comes to listening. If you aren't as skilled at listening as you would like to be, then the first thing to do to improve your ability is to be aware of common barriers to listening:

Overvaluing Talking

A comic once described listening as being "composed of the rude interruptions between my exclamations." Many people's attitudes about listening agree with that statement more than they would like to admit. For example, if you asked six people how they could improve their communication skills, most of them would describe the need to become more persuasive or sharpen their public speaking skills. Few would cite a desire to listen better.

Most people overvalue talking and undervalue listening, even those in people-related jobs, such as sales. But the truth is that effective communication is not persuasion. It's listening. Think about it: Nobody ever *listened* himself or herself out of a sale.

Good communicators know to monitor their talking-to-listening ratio. President Abraham Lincoln, considered one of the most effective leaders and communicators in our nation's history, said, "When I'm getting ready to reason with a man, I spend one third of my time thinking about myself and what I am going to say—and two thirds thinking about him and what he is going to say." That's a good ratio to maintain. Listen twice as much as you speak.

Lacking Focus

For some people, especially those with high energy, slowing down enough to really listen can be challenging. Most people tend to speak about 180 words a minute, but they can listen at 300 to 500 words a minute. That disparity can create tension and cause a listener to lose focus. Most people try to fill up that communication gap by finding other things to do, such as daydream, think about their daily schedule or mentally review their to-do list, or watch other people. It's similar to what we do when we drive a car. We rarely just watch the road and do nothing else. Usually we look at the scenery, eat and drink, talk, or listen to the radio.

If you want to become a better listener, however, you need to learn to direct that energy and attention positively by concentrating on the person you're with. Observe body language. Watch for changes in facial expression. Look into the person's eyes. Management expert Peter Drucker remarked, "The most important thing in communication is to hear what isn't being said." If you expend your extra energy by observing the other person closely and interpreting what he or she says, your listening skills will improve dramatically.

Experiencing Mental Fatigue

Former president Ronald Reagan told an amusing story about two psychiatrists, one older and one younger. Each day they showed up at work immaculately dressed and alert. But at the end of the day, the younger doctor was frazzled and disheveled while the older man was as fresh as ever.

"How do you do it?" the younger psychiatrist finally asked his colleague. "You always stay so fresh after hearing patients all day."

The older doctor replied, "It's easy. I never listen."[1]

Whenever you listen to others for extended periods of time, the effect can be exhausting. But any kind of mental fatigue can negatively affect your ability to listen.

We heard a story about an eighty-nine-year-old woman with hearing problems. She visited her doctor, and after examining her, he said, "We now have a procedure that can correct your hearing problem. When would you like to schedule the operation?"

"There won't be any operation, because I don't want my hearing corrected," said the woman. "I'm eighty-nine years old, and I've heard enough!"

If you're tired or facing difficult circumstances, remember that to remain an effective listener, you have to dig up more energy, concentrate, and stay focused.

Stereotyping

Stereotyping others can be a huge barrier to listening. It tends to make us hear what we expect rather than what another person actually says. Most of us may think that we don't fall into this trap, but we all do to some degree. Read the following humorous list of stereotype breakers from a piece called "Things I'd Like to Hear—But Won't" created by David Grimes. If you never expect to hear any of these things from the people listed, then you may be guilty of stereotyping:

From my auto mechanic:
"That part is much less expensive than I thought."
"You could get that done more cheaply at the garage down the street."
"It was just a loose wire. No charge."

From a store clerk:
"The computerized cash register is down. I'll just add up your purchases with a pencil and paper."
"I'll take a break *after* I finish waiting on these customers."
"We're sorry we sold you defective merchandise. We'll pick it up at your home and bring you a new one or give you a complete refund, whichever you prefer."

From a contractor:
"Whoever worked on this before sure knew what he was doing."
"I think I came in a little high on that estimate."

From the dentist:
"I think you're flossing too much."
"I won't ask you any questions until I take the pick out of your mouth."

From a restaurant server:
"I think it's presumptuous for a waiter to volunteer his name, but since you ask, it's Tim."
"I was slow and inattentive. I cannot accept any tip."[2]

These statements are clever. And they are also a reminder that it's a bad idea to stereotype others. Whenever you treat people strictly as members of a group rather than as individuals, you can get into trouble. So watch out. If you talk to people and find yourself thinking of them as computer geeks, typical teenagers, ditsy blondes, stiff engineer types, or some other representative of a group instead of as individual people, beware. You may not really be listening to what they have to say.

Carrying Personal Emotional Baggage

Nearly everyone has emotional filters that prevent him or her from hearing certain things that other people say. Your past experiences, both positive and negative, color the way you look at life and shape your expectations. And particularly strong experiences, such as traumas or incidents from childhood, can make you tend to react strongly whenever you perceive you are in a similar situation. As Mark Twain once said, "A cat who sits on a hot stove will never sit on a hot stove again. He'll never sit on a cold stove either. From then on, that cat just won't like stoves."

If you've never worked through strong past emotional experiences, you may be filtering what others say through those experiences. If you're preoccupied with certain topics, if a particular subject makes you defensive, or if you frequently project your point of view onto others, you may need to work through your issues before you can become an effective listener.

Sigmund Freud stated, "A man with a toothache cannot be in love," meaning that the toothache doesn't allow him to notice anything other than his pain. Similarly, anytime a person has an ax to grind, the words of others are drowned out by the sound of the grindstone.

Being Preoccupied with Self

Probably the most formidable barrier to listening is preoccupation with self. Many years ago we saw a TV sketch that illustrates this point really well. A husband was watching television, and his wife was trying to engage him in conversation:

WIFE: Dear, the plumber didn't make it in time to fix the leak by the hot water heater today.

HUSBAND: Uh-huh.

WIFE: So the pipe burst and flooded the basement.

HUSBAND: Quiet. It's third down and goal to go.

WIFE: Some of the wiring got wet and almost electrocuted Fluffy.

HUSBAND: Oh, no, they've got a man open. Shoot! Touchdown.

WIFE: The vet says he'll be better in a week.

HUSBAND: Can you get me something to eat?

WIFE: The plumber finally came and said that he was happy our pipe broke because now he can afford to go on vacation.

HUSBAND: Aren't you *listening*? I said I'm hungry!

WIFE: And, Stanley, I'm leaving you. The plumber and I are flying to Acapulco in the morning.

HUSBAND: Can't you please stop all that yakking and get me something to eat? The trouble around here is that nobody ever listens to me.

If you don't care about anyone but yourself, you're not going to listen to others. But the ironic thing is that when you don't listen, the damage you do to yourself is ultimately even greater than what you do to other people.

How to Develop Listening Skills

According to Brian Adams, author of *Sales Cybernetics*, during the average waking day, we spend most of it listening. He offers the following statistics:

>   9 percent of the day is spent writing
> 16 percent of the day is spent reading
> 30 percent of the day is spent speaking
> 45 percent of the day is spent *listening*[3]

So you probably agree that listening is important. But what does it mean to listen? We heard a story about a high school music appreciation class that provides a meaningful answer to that question. The teacher of the class asked for a volunteer to explain the difference between listening and hearing. At first no one wanted to answer, but finally, a student raised his hand. When the teacher called on him, he said, "Listening is *wanting* to hear."

That answer is a great start. To become a good listener, you have to want to hear. But you also need some skills to help you. Here are nine suggestions to help you become a better listener:

1. Look at the Speaker

The whole listening process begins with giving the other person your undivided attention. As you interact with someone, don't catch up on other work, shuffle papers, do the dishes, or watch television. Set aside the time to focus only on the other person. And if you don't have the time at that moment, then schedule it as soon as you can.

2. Don't Interrupt

Most people react badly to being interrupted. It makes them feel disrespected. And according to Robert L. Montgomery, author of *Listening Made Easy,* "It's just as rude to step on people's ideas as it is to step on their toes."

People who tend to interrupt others generally do so for one of these reasons:

- They don't place enough value on what the other person has to say.
- They want to impress others by showing how smart or intuitive they are.
- They're too excited by the conversation to let the other person finish talking.

If you are in the habit of interrupting other people, examine your motives and determine to make a change. Give people the time they need to express themselves. And don't feel that one of you has to be speaking all the time. Periods of silence give you a chance to reflect on what's been said so that you can respond appropriately.

3. Focus on Understanding

Have you ever noticed how quickly most people forget the things they hear? Studies at institutions such as Michigan State, Ohio State, Florida State, and the University of Minnesota indicate that most people can recall only 50 percent of what they hear immediately after hearing it. And as time passes, their ability to remember continues to drop. By the next day, their retention is usually down to about 25 percent.

One way to combat that tendency is to make your goal understanding rather than just remembering facts. Lawyer, lecturer, and author Herb Cohen emphasized, "Effective listening requires more than hearing the words transmitted. It demands that you find meaning and understanding in what is being said. After all, meanings are not in words, but in people."

To increase your understanding of others as you listen, follow these guidelines offered by Eric Allenbaugh:

1. Listen with a head-heart connection.
2. Listen with the intent of understanding.
3. Listen for the message and the message behind the message.
4. Listen for both content and feelings.
5. Listen with your eyes—your hearing will be improved.
6. Listen for others' interest, not just their position.
7. Listen for what they are saying and not saying.
8. Listen with empathy and acceptance.
9. Listen for the areas where they are afraid and hurt.
10. Listen as you would like to be listened to.[4]

As you learn to put yourself in the other person's place, your ability to understand will increase. And the greater your ability to understand, the better listener you will become.

4.   Determine the Need at the Moment

The ability to discern the other person's need at the moment is part of becoming an effective listener. People talk for so many different reasons: to receive comfort, to vent, to persuade, to inform, to be understood, or to relieve nervousness. Often people talk to you for reasons that don't match your expectations.

A lot of men and women find themselves in conflict because they occasionally communicate at cross-purposes. They neglect to determine the need of the other person at the moment of interaction. Men usually want to fix any problems they discuss; their need is resolution. Women, on the other hand, are more likely to tell about a problem simply to share it; they often neither request nor desire solutions. Anytime you can determine the current need of the people you're communicating with, you can put whatever they say into the appropriate context. And you will be better able to understand them.

5.   Check Your Emotions

As we've already mentioned, most people carry around emotional baggage that causes them to react to certain people or situations. Anytime that you become highly emotional when listening to another person, check your emotions—especially if your reaction seems to be stronger than the situation warrants. You don't want to make an unsuspecting person the recipient of your venting. Besides, even if your reactions are not due to an event from your past, you should always allow others to finish explaining their points of view, ideas, or convictions before offering your own.

6.   Suspend Your Judgment

Have you ever begun listening to another person tell a story and started to respond to it before he or she was finished? Just about everyone has. But the truth is that you can't jump to conclusions and be a good listener at the same time. As you talk to others, wait to hear the whole story before you respond. If you don't, you may miss the most important thing they intend to say.

7. Sum Up at Major Intervals

Experts agree that listening is most effective when it's active. John H. Melchinger suggests, "Comment on what you hear, and individualize your comments. For example, you can say, 'Cheryl, that's obviously very important to you.' It will help keep you on track as a listener. Get beyond, 'That's interesting.' If you train yourself to comment meaningfully, the speaker will know you are listening and may offer further information."

A technique for active listening is to sum up what the other person says at major intervals. As the speaker finishes one subject, paraphrase his or her main points or ideas before going on to the next one, and verify that you have gotten the right message. Doing that reassures the person and helps you stay focused on what he or she is trying to communicate.

8. Ask Questions for Clarity

Have you ever noticed that top reporters are excellent listeners? Take someone like Barbara Walters, for example. She looks at the speaker, focuses on understanding, suspends judgment, and sums up what the person has to say. People trust her and seem to be willing to tell her just about anything. But she practices another skill that helps her to gather more information and increase her understanding of the person she is interviewing. She asks good questions.

If you want to become an effective listener, become a good reporter—not a stick-the-microphone-in-your-face-and-bark-questions-at-you reporter, but someone who gently asks follow-up questions and seeks clarification. If you show people how much you care and ask in a nonthreatening way, you'll be amazed by how much they'll tell you.

9. *Always Make Listening Your Priority*

The last thing to remember when developing your listening skills is to make listening a priority, no matter how busy you become or how far you rise in your organization. A remarkable example of a busy executive who made time for listening was the late Sam Walton, founder of Wal-Mart and one of the richest men in America. He believed in listening to what people had to say, especially his employees. He once flew his plane to Mt. Pleasant, Texas, landed, and gave instructions to his copilot to meet him about one hundred miles down the road. He then rode in a Wal-Mart truck the rest of the way just so that he could chat with the driver. We should all give listening that kind of priority.

---

*If you show people how much you care and ask
questions in a nonthreatening way, you'll
be amazed by how much they'll tell you.*

Many people take for granted the ability to listen. Most people consider listening to be easy, and they view themselves as pretty good listeners. But while it's true that most people are able to hear, fewer are capable of really listening.

In our careers, we have done a lot of speaking. Between the two of us, we speak to several hundred thousand people every year. Jim's wife, Nancy, does a lot of speaking—and believe us, she is a great talker! But she is also a wonderful listener, and sometimes when she speaks, she talks about communication and the importance of listening. Not long ago she gave a talk about listening that emphasized giving other people the benefit of the doubt and trying to see things from their point of view.

In the audience that day was a man named Rodney. Though he was happily married and had a young son, he had been previously married and had two daughters with his first wife. And he was having problems with her. She was constantly calling him and asking for more money for herself and the two girls. They argued continually, and she was driving him so nuts that he had already hired an attorney and was preparing to sue her.

But when Rodney heard Nancy speak about listening that day, he realized how insensitive he had been to his ex-wife, Charlotte. A couple of days later he called her and asked if they could meet. She was suspicious of Rodney and even asked her attorney to call him to find out what he was up to. But eventually, Rodney convinced them that he just wanted to talk, and finally, Charlotte agreed to see him.

They met at a coffee shop, and Rodney said, "Charlotte, I want to listen to you. Tell me what your life is like. I do care about you and the kids."

"I didn't think you cared about the girls at all," she said as she began to cry.

"I do," he said. "I'm sorry. I've only been thinking of myself, and I haven't been thinking of you. Please forgive me."

"Why are you doing this?" she asked.

"Because I want to make things right," he answered. "I've been angry for so long that I couldn't see straight. Now, tell me how things are going for you and the girls."

For a while, Charlotte could only sob. But then she started telling him about her struggles as a single parent and how she was doing her best to bring up the girls, but that it didn't seem like enough. They talked for hours, and as they did, the beginning of a new foundation of mutual respect formed. In time, they believe they will be able to become friends again.

Rodney is probably not alone. Can you think of people you haven't been listening to lately? And what are you going to do about it? It's never too late to become a good listener. It can change your life—and the lives of the people in your life.

Influence Checklist
LISTENING TO PEOPLE

❏ **Measure your listening skills.** Have someone who knows you well use the following questions to evaluate your listening skills according to the nine qualities of good listening discussed in this chapter. Ask him or her to explain any no answers. And don't interrupt or defend yourself as you receive the explanation.

1. Do I usually look at the speaker while he or she is talking?
2. Do I wait for the speaker to finish talking before I respond?
3. Do I make understanding my goal?
4. Am I usually sensitive to the speaker's immediate need?
5. Do I make it a practice to check my emotions?
6. Do I regularly suspend my judgment until I get the whole story?
7. Am I in the practice of summing up what the speaker says at major intervals?
8. Do I ask questions for clarity when needed?
9. Do I communicate to others that listening is a priority?

❏ **Strategy for improvement.** Based on the answers received, list three ways you could improve your listening skills:
1._____
2._____
3._____

Commit yourself to making those improvements during the coming weeks.

❏ **Schedule a listening occasion.** Make an appointment with the most important person in your life this week, and plan to spend an hour together just communicating. Give that person your undivided attention, and spend at least two-thirds of the time just listening to him or her.

CHAPTER 5

A Person of Influence . . .

UNDERSTANDS PEOPLE

MULTIPLY

MENTOR

MOTIVATE—*Understand*

MODEL

The other night over dinner, the two of us were talking, and we started to explore some questions. How does a person build an organization? What does it take? What is the key to being successful? For example, what did it take for a person like Jim to build a business organization that's active in twenty-six countries and impacts the lives of hundreds of thousands of people? Or in the case of John, what did it take to triple the size of his church—making it the largest in its denomination—and in the process increase its budget from around $800,000 to more than $5 million, and raise active involvement by volunteers from just 112 to more than 1,800 people?

It doesn't matter whether your business is creating computer software, selling books, serving food in a restaurant, building houses, or designing airplanes. The key to success is understanding people. Jim says,

I'm not like John. I didn't grow up with an orientation toward people. He took Dale Carnegie courses while he was still in high school and went off to college knowing he would be in a people job. I went to Purdue University and studied aeronautical engineering. By the time I finished with my bachelor's degree, I thought there were two keys to success in any job: hard work and technical skills. It never even occurred to me that people skills had any value.

I entered my first job ready to work and loaded with technical knowledge. Purdue had given me a first-rate education, and I had always believed in working hard. But it didn't take me long to realize that success in business means being able to work with people. In fact, all of life is dealing with people. I found that to be true not only professionally as an engineer, a consultant, and an entrepreneur, but in every aspect of living, whether I was interacting with my family, working with one of my kids' teachers, or socializing with friends.

If you can't understand people and work with them, you can't accomplish anything. And you certainly can't become a person of influence.

Understanding People
Pays Great Dividends

In *Climbing the Executive Ladder,* authors Kienzle and Dare said, "Few things will pay you bigger dividends than the time and trouble you take to understand people. Almost nothing will add more to your stature as an executive and a person. Nothing will give you greater satisfaction or bring you more happiness."

> *When we understand the other fellow's
> viewpoint—understand what he is trying
> to do—nine times out of ten he is
> trying to do right.*
> —*Harry Truman*

The ability to understand people is one of the greatest assets anyone can ever have. It has the potential to positively impact every area of your life, not just the business arena. For example, look at how understanding people helped this mother of a preschooler. She said,

Leaving my four-year-old son in the house, I ran out to throw something in the trash. When I tried to open the door to get back inside, it was locked. I knew that insisting that my son open the door would have resulted in an hour-long battle of the wills. So in a sad voice, I said, "Oh, too bad. You just locked yourself in the house." The door opened at once.

Understanding people certainly impacts your ability to communicate with others. David Burns, a medical doctor and professor of psychiatry at the University of Pennsylvania, observed, "The biggest mistake you can make in trying to talk convincingly is to put your highest priority on expressing your ideas and feelings. What most people really want is to be listened to, respected, and understood. The moment people see that they are being understood, they become more motivated to understand your point of view." If you can learn to understand people—how they think, what they feel, what inspires them, how they're likely to act and react in a given situation—then you can motivate and influence them in a positive way.

WHY PEOPLE FAIL TO UNDERSTAND OTHERS

Lack of understanding concerning others is a recurrent source of tension in our society. We once heard an attorney say, "Half of all the controversies and conflicts that arise among people are caused not by differences of opinion or an inability to agree, but by their lack of understanding for one another." If we could just reduce the number of misunderstandings, the courts wouldn't be as crowded, there would be fewer violent crimes, the divorce rate would go down, and the amount of everyday stress most people experience would drop dramatically.

If understanding is such an asset, why don't more people practice it? There are many reasons:

Fear

Seventeenth-century American colonist William Penn advised, "Neither despise or oppose what thou dost not understand," yet many people seem to do exactly that. When they don't understand others, they often react by becoming fearful. And once they start fearing others, they rarely try to overcome their fear in order to learn more about them. It becomes a vicious cycle.

Unfortunately, fear is evident in the workplace when it comes to employees' reactions toward their leaders. Laborers fear their managers. Middle managers are intimidated by senior managers. Both groups are sometimes afraid of executives. The whole situation causes undue suspicion, lack of communication, and reduced productivity. For example, according to Dr. M. Michael Markowich, vice president of human resources at United Hospitals, Inc., employees are reluctant to suggest ideas. Here are some reasons why:

- They think their ideas will be rejected.
- They feel coworkers won't like the ideas.
- They think they won't get credit if the ideas work.
- They're afraid the boss will be threatened by the ideas.
- They're concerned that they'll be labeled as troublemakers.
- They're afraid of losing their jobs if they suggest ideas that don't work.[1]

The common thread in all of these reasons is fear. Yet in a healthy work environment, if you give others the benefit of the doubt and replace fear with understanding, everyone can work together positively. All people have to do is follow the advice of President Harry Truman, who said, "When we understand the other fellow's viewpoint—understand what he is trying to do—nine times out of ten he is trying to do right."

Self-Centeredness

When fear isn't a stumbling block to understanding, self-centeredness often is. Someone remarked, "There are two sides to every question—as long as it doesn't concern us personally." That's the way too many people think. Everyone is not self-centered on purpose; it's just in the nature of people to think of their own interests first. If you want to see an example of that, play with a two-year-old child. He naturally chooses the best toys for himself and insists on his own way.

One way to overcome our natural self-centeredness is to try to see things from other people's perspectives. Talking to a group of salespeople, Art Mortell shared this experience: "Whenever I'm losing at chess, I consistently get up and stand behind my opponent and see the board from his side. Then I start to discover the stupid moves I've made because I can see it from his viewpoint. The salesperson's challenge is to see the world from the prospect's viewpoint."[2]

That's the challenge for every one of us, no matter what our profession. There is a quote that John filed away years ago called "A Short Course in Human Relations." You may have already heard it because it's been around for a while. But it reminds us of what our priorities should be when dealing with other people:

The least important word: I
The most important word: We
The two most important words: Thank you.
The three most important words: All is forgiven.
The four most important words: What is your opinion?
The five most important words: You did a good job.
The six most important words: I want to understand you better.

Changing your attitude from self-centeredness to understanding requires desire and commitment to always try to see things from the other person's point of view.

Failure to Appreciate Differences

The next logical step after leaving behind self-centeredness is learning to recognize and respect everyone else's unique qualities. Instead of trying to cast others in your image, learn to appreciate their differences. If someone has a talent that you don't have, great. The two of you can strengthen each other's weaknesses. If others come from a different culture, broaden your horizons and learn what you can from them. Your new knowledge will help you relate not only to them, but also to others. And celebrate people's differences in temperament. Variety makes for interesting dynamics between people. For instance, John has a choleric-sanguine temperament, which means he loves to have fun and enjoys making decisions in the blink of an eye. On the other hand, Jim is a melancholy-phlegmatic. He is a great thinker and processor of information, and when he needs to make decisions, he gathers as much data as he can to make wise choices. Separate, we do well. But we're even more effective when the two of us are together.

Once you learn to appreciate other people's differences, you come to realize that there are many responses to leadership and motivation. Joseph Beck, the president of the Kenley Corporation, recognized that truth when he said that an influencer "must realize that different people are motivated in different ways. A good basketball coach, for example, knows when a player needs encouragement to excel and when a player needs a 'kick in the pants.' The main difference is that all players need encouragement and only some need a 'kick in the pants.'"

Failure to Acknowledge Similarities

As you learn more about people and get to know others well, you soon begin to realize that people have a lot in common. We all have hopes and fears, joys and sorrows, victories and problems. Probably the time when people are least likely to recognize their common ground with others is during adolescence. We came across a story that illustrates this:

> A teenage girl was talking to her father about all of her problems. She told him of the terrible peer pressure she faced, about conflicts with friends, and difficulties with schoolwork and teachers. In an attempt to help her put everything in perspective, he told her that life was not as dark as it might seem and, in fact, much of her worry was perhaps unnecessary.
>
> "That's easy for you to say, Dad," she replied. "You already have all your problems over with."

All people have an emotional reaction to what's happening around them. To foster understanding, think of what *your* emotions would be if you were in the same position as the person you're interacting with. You know what you would want to happen in a given situation. Chances are that the person you're working with has many of the same feelings.

We found a wonderful example of a person who understands this approach. A candy store sold its exotic chocolates only by the pound. In the store was one particular salesclerk who always had customers lined up waiting while other salesclerks stood around with nothing to do. The owner of the store noticed how the customers flocked to her and finally asked for her secret.

"It's easy," she said. "The other girls scoop up more than a pound of candy and then start taking away. I always scoop up less than a pound and then add to it. The customers feel that I'm looking out for them and getting them their money's worth."

THINGS EVERYBODY NEEDS TO UNDERSTAND ABOUT PEOPLE

Knowing what people need and want is the key to understanding them. And if you can understand them, you can influence them and impact their lives in a positive way. If we were to boil down all the things we know about understanding people and narrow them down to a short list, we would identify these five things:

1. *Everybody Wants to Be Somebody*

There isn't a person in the world who doesn't have the desire to be someone, to have significance. Even the least ambitious and unassuming person wants to be regarded highly by others.

John remembers the first time these feelings were stirred strongly within him. It was back when he was in the fourth grade:

I went to my first basketball game when I was nine years old. I can still see it in my head. I stood with my buddies in the balcony of the gym. The thing that I remember most wasn't the game; it was the announcement of the starting lineups. They turned all the lights out, and then some spotlights came on. The announcer called out the names of the starters, and they ran out to the middle of the floor one by one with everybody in the place cheering.

I hung over the balcony that day as a fourth-grade kid and said, "Wow, I'd like that to happen to me." In fact, by the time the introductions were over, I looked at my friend Bobby Wilson, and I said,

"Bobby, when I get to high school, they're going to announce my name, and I'm going to run out in the spotlight to the middle of that basketball floor. And the people are going to cheer for me because I'm going to become somebody."

I went home that night and told my dad, "I want to be a basketball player." Soon afterward, he got me a Spalding basketball, and we put a goal on the garage. I used to shovel snow off that driveway to practice my foul shots and play basketball, because I had a dream of becoming somebody.

It's funny how that kind of dream can impact your life. I remember in sixth grade we played intramural basketball, and our team won a couple of games, so we got to go to the Old Mill Street Gym in Circleville, Ohio, where I'd seen that basketball game in the fourth grade. When we got there, instead of going out onto the floor with the rest of the players as they were warming up, I went over to the bench where those high school players had been two years before. I sat right where they had, and I closed my eyes (the equivalent of turning the lights out in the gym). Then in my head I heard my name announced, and I ran out in the middle of the floor.

It felt so good to hear that imaginary applause that I thought, *I'll do it again!* So I did. In fact, I did it three times, and all of a sudden I realized that my buddies weren't playing basketball; they were just watching me in disbelief. But I didn't even care because I was one step closer to being the person I'd dreamed about becoming.

Everybody wants to be regarded and valued by others. In other words, everybody wants to be somebody. Once that piece of information becomes a part of your everyday thinking, you'll gain incredible insight into why people do the things they do. And if you treat every person you meet as if he or she were the most important person in the world, you'll communicate that he or she *is* somebody—to you.

2. *Nobody Cares How Much You Know Until He Knows How Much You Care*

To be an influencer, you have to love people before you try to lead them. The moment that people know that you care for and about them, the way they feel about you changes.

Showing others that you care isn't always easy. Your greatest times and fondest memories will come because of people, but so will your most difficult, hurting, and tragic times. People are your greatest assets and your greatest liabilities. The challenge is to keep caring about them no matter what.

We came across something called "Paradoxical Commandments of Leadership." Here's what it says:

People are illogical, unreasonable, and self-centered—love them anyway.

If you do good, people will accuse you of selfish ulterior motives—do good anyway.

If you're successful, you'll win false friends and true enemies—succeed anyway.

The good you do today will perhaps be forgotten tomorrow—do good anyway.

Honesty and frankness make you vulnerable—be honest and frank anyway.

The biggest man with the biggest ideas can be shot down by the smallest man with the smallest mind—think big anyway.

People favor underdogs but follow only hot dogs—fight for the few underdogs anyway.

What you spend years building may be destroyed overnight—build anyway.

People really need help but may attack you if you help them—help them anyway.

Give the world the best that you have and you will get kicked in the teeth—give the world the best that you have anyway.[3]

If better is possible, then good is not enough.

If you want to help others and become a person of influence, keep smiling, sharing, giving, and turning the other cheek. That's the right way to treat people. Besides, you never know which people in your sphere of influence are going to rise up and make a difference in your life and the lives of others.

3. Everybody Needs Somebody

Contrary to popular belief, there are no such things as self-made men and women. Everybody needs friendship, encouragement, and help. What people can accomplish by themselves is almost nothing compared to their potential when working with others. And doing things with other people tends to bring contentment. Besides, Lone Rangers are rarely happy people. King Solomon of ancient Israel stated the value of working together this way:

> Two are better than one,
>   because they have a good return for their work:
> If one falls down,
>   his friend can help him up.
> But pity the man who falls
>   and has no one to help him up!
> Also, if two lie down together, they will keep warm.
>   But how can one keep warm alone?
> Though one may be overpowered,
>   two can defend themselves.
> A cord of three strands is not quickly broken.[4]

People who try to do everything alone often get themselves into trouble. One of the wildest stories we've ever seen on this subject came from the insurance claim form of a bricklayer who got hurt at a building site. He was trying to get a load of bricks down from the top floor of a building without asking for help from anyone else. He wrote:

> It would have taken too long to carry all the bricks down by hand, so I decided to put them in a barrel and lower them by a pulley which I had fastened to the top of the building. After tying the rope securely at ground level, I then went up to the top of the building, I fastened the rope around the barrel, loaded it with bricks, and swung it over the sidewalk for the descent. Then I went down to the sidewalk and untied the rope, holding it securely to guide the barrel down slowly. But since I weigh only 140 pounds, the 500-pound load jerked me from the ground so fast that I didn't have time to think of letting go of the rope. As I passed between the second and third floors I met the barrel coming down. This accounts for the bruises and the lacerations on my upper body.
>
> I held tightly to the rope until I reached the top, where my hand became jammed in the pulley. This accounts for my broken thumb.
>
> At the same time, however, the barrel hit the sidewalk with a bang and the bottom fell out. With the weight of the bricks gone, the barrel weighed only about 40 pounds. Thus my 140-pound body began a swift descent, and I met the empty barrel coming up. This accounts for my broken ankle.
>
> Slowed only slightly, I continued the descent and landed on the pile of bricks. This accounts for my sprained back and broken collarbone.
>
> At this point I lost my presence of mind completely, and I let go of the rope and the empty barrel came crashing down on me. This accounts for my head injuries.
>
> And as for the last question on your insurance form, "What would I do if the same situation rose again?" Please be advised I am finished trying to do the job all by myself.

Everybody needs somebody to come alongside and help. If you understand that, are willing to give to others and help them, and maintain the right motives, their lives and yours can change.

*4. Everybody Can Be Somebody When Somebody Understands
     and Believes in Her*

Once you understand people and believe in them, they really can
become somebody. And it doesn't take much effort to help other people
feel important. Little things, done deliberately at the right time, can make
a big difference, as this story from John shows:

> For fourteen years, I was privileged to pastor a very large congrega-
> tion in the San Diego area where we did a wonderful Christmas pro-
> gram every year. We used to do twenty-eight performances, and
> altogether about thirty thousand people saw it each year.
>
> The show always included a bunch of kids, and one of my favorite
> parts of the show several years ago was a song in which three hundred
> kids dressed like angels sang while holding candles. Toward the end of
> the song, they walked off the stage, came up the aisles, and exited out
> of the lobby in the front of the church.
>
> During the first performance, I decided to wait for them back in the
> lobby. They didn't know I was going to be there, but as they went by I
> clapped, praised them, and said, "Kids, you did a great job!" They were
> surprised to see me, and they were glad for the encouragement.
>
> For the second performance, I did the same thing again. And I could
> see as they started to walk up the aisles, they were looking back expec-
> tantly to see if I was standing there to cheer them on. By the third per-
> formance of the night, as they turned the corner to come up the aisle,
> they had smiles on their faces. And when they got to the lobby, they
> were giving me high fives and having a great time. They knew I
> believed in them, and it made all of them feel that they were somebody.

When was the last time you went out of your way to make people feel
special, as if they were somebody? The investment required on your part
is totally overshadowed by the impact it makes on them. Everyone you
know and all the people you meet have the potential to be someone
important in the lives of others. All they need is encouragement and
motivation from you to help them reach their potential.

5.   *Anybody Who Helps Somebody Influences a Lot of Bodies*

The final thing you need to understand about people is that when you help one person, you're really impacting a lot of other people. What you give to one person overflows into the lives of all the people that person impacts. The nature of influence is to multiply. It even impacts you because when you help others and your motives are good, you always receive more than you can ever give. Most people are so genuinely grateful when another person makes them feel that they're somebody special that they never tire of showing their gratitude.

CHOOSE TO UNDERSTAND OTHERS

In the end, the ability to understand people is a choice. It's true that some people are born with great instincts that enable them to understand how others think and feel. But even if you aren't an instinctive people person, you can improve your ability to work with others. Every person is capable of having the ability to understand, motivate, and ultimately influence others.

If you truly want to make a difference in the lives of others, then make up your mind to possess . . .

The Other Person's Perspective

Mark McCormack, author of *What They Don't Teach You at Harvard Business School,* wrote about an amusing story for *Entrepreneur* magazine. It illustrates the value of recognizing other people's perspectives. He said, "A few years ago I was standing in an airport ticket line. In front of me were two children fighting over an ice cream cone. In front of them was a woman in a mink coat. I could see this was an accident waiting to happen. Should I interfere? I was still pondering this when I heard the girl tell the boy, 'If you don't stop, Charlie, you'll get hairs from that lady's coat on your cone.'"

Most people don't look beyond their own experience when dealing with others. They tend to see other people and events in the context of their own position, background, or circumstances. For example, Pat McInally of the NFL's Cincinnati Bengals said, "At Harvard they labeled me a jock. In the pros they consider me an intellectual." Though he had not changed, other people's perceptions of him had.

Whenever you look at things from the other person's perspective, you'll receive a whole new way of looking at life. And you'll find new ways of helping others. A story from the book *Zadig* by Voltaire shows the value of looking at people and situations in a new way.

A country's ruler was upset because his favorite horse was missing. The king sent couriers throughout the land to look for it, but to no avail. In desperation, the king offered a great reward. Many came hoping to win it and searched for the horse, but they all failed. The horse had disappeared.

A simpleton at the king's court sought an audience with the monarch and told him that he could find the horse.

"You!" exclaimed the king. "You can find my horse when all others have failed?"

"Yes, sire," answered the simpleton.

"Then do it," said the king, who had nothing to lose.

Within hours the horse was back at the palace, and the king was astounded. He immediately had his treasurer issue a handsome reward to the man, and asked him to explain how he had found it when many men considered wise had not.

"It was easy, sire," said the simpleton. "I merely asked myself, 'If I was a horse, where would I go?' And putting myself in his place, I soon found him."

Personal Empathy

Another quality that you need if you want to understand and help others is personal empathy. Not everyone is naturally empathetic, as is evident in this story about a Kansas preacher. It seems that the preacher was returning home after a visit to New England, and one of his parishioners met him at the train station.

"Well," asked the preacher, "how are things at home?"

"Sad, real sad, Pastor," answered the man. "A cyclone came and wiped out my house."

"Well, I'm not surprised," said the unsympathetic parson with a frown. "You remember I've been warning you about the way you've been living. Punishment for sin is inevitable."

"It also destroyed your house, Pastor," added the layman.

"It did?" the pastor said, momentarily surprised. "Ah, me, the ways of the Lord are past human understanding."

Don't wait for your house to be blown down to have feelings about people's troubles and shortcomings. Reach out to others with a strong hand but a soft heart, and they'll respond to you positively.

A Positive Attitude About People

Author Harper Lee wrote, "People generally see what they look for and hear what they listen for." If you have a positive attitude about people, believe the best of them, and act on your beliefs, then you can have an impact on their lives. But it all starts with the way you think of others. You can't be a positive influencer if your thinking is like this:

When the other fellow takes a long time, he's slow.
> When I take a long time, I'm thorough.

When the other fellow doesn't do it, he's lazy.
> When I don't do it, I'm busy.

When the other fellow does something without being told, he's overstepping his bounds.
> When I do it, that's initiative.

When the other fellow overlooks a rule of etiquette, he's rude.
> When I skip a few rules, I'm original.

When the other fellow pleases the boss, he's an apple polisher.
> When I please the boss, it's cooperation.

When the other fellow gets ahead, he's getting the breaks.
> When I manage to get ahead, that's just the reward for hard work.

Your attitude toward people is one of the most important choices you'll ever make. If your thinking is positive, you can really make an impact on them. Pastor Robert Schuller, a strong proponent of positive thinking, tells the following story in *Life Changers:*

"I'm the greatest baseball player in the world," the little boy boasted as he strutted around his backyard. Shouldering his bat, he tossed a baseball up, swung, and missed. "I am the greatest ball player ever," he reiterated. He picked up the ball again, swung, and missed again. Stopping a moment to examine his bat, he stooped and picked up his ball. "I am the greatest baseball player who ever lived!" The momentum of his swing nearly knocked him down. But the ball plopped, unscathed, at his feet. "Wow!" he exclaimed. "What a pitcher!"[5]

If you want to become a person of influence, have an attitude toward others similar to the attitude that little boy had about himself.

> *If you treat every person you meet*
> *as if he or she were the most important*
> *person in the world, you'll communicate*
> *that he or she is somebody—to you.*

Jim was reminded of the importance of understanding people and seeing things from their perspective when visiting his aging parents in New York recently:

My parents are in their upper eighties, and they worked hard all their lives. My dad was the city editor of the Niagara Falls *Gazette,* and my mother was the night supervising nurse at Niagara Falls Memorial Hospital. She worked many years from 11 PM to 7 AM when I was young so that she could be home to get me up for school, make breakfast, and pack my lunch. And then she was there when I got home from school each afternoon. I hardly realized she worked. Growing up we always lived in a very small house. After they retired, they sold it and moved to a small apartment to live on their modest pensions.

Like most people who have been blessed financially, Nancy and I are always looking for ways to help our parents and repay them in some small way for the positive things they have done for us over the years. Recently, we thought we could help them by leasing them a penthouse unit in the most prestigious apartment building in the city. It was incredible and even had a view of Niagara Falls.

But after about six months, my parents asked if they could move out. My mother's eyesight was now so poor that she couldn't see the Falls. Dad, on the other hand, could see the Falls fine but was made extremely uncomfortable by being up so high. We were disappointed that they didn't like it, but we readily agreed to move them back into their small apartment.

My desire to help them was still strong, so one day after we got them squared away in their place, I took Mom to the store. Though she claimed she didn't need anything, I did manage to talk her into letting me get her a few items: a new trash can, some flatware, a small radio, and a new toaster—the old one had *shot* the toast out like a cannon when it was done. And it made me feel good when I overheard her showing the toaster to a neighbor and saying, "My *son* bought this for us!"

Nancy and I had wanted to get them big things, but that's not what was important to them. They were happy with a toaster. Oh, yes, there was one other item they finally admitted that they could use: a small tree for the front of their apartment. They thought it would be nice to have some shade in the summer when they sat outside. "But they're so expensive," my mother said. "Just get us a sapling."

We wanted them to have shade *today*, not fifteen years from now. So we went out and got them the biggest tree we could find. It didn't take a lot of money to make them happy, just a little understanding.

Not everyone learns that lesson. Lots of people try to push their own agenda—and then they wonder why they have no pull with others. To make an impact on others, find out what people want and then help them get it. That's what motivates them. And that's what makes it possible for you to become a person of influence in their lives.

Influence Checklist

UNDERSTANDING PEOPLE

❏ **Rate your understanding.** Use the following scale to rate your ability to understand people (circle the rating that applies to you):

Superior   I can nearly always anticipate how people will feel and react in any given situation. Understanding is one of my strongest abilities.

Good   Most of the time what people do and want makes sense to me. I consider my ability to understand people an asset.

Fair   I'm surprised by people just as often as I'm able to anticipate their thinking. I consider my ability to understand others to be average.

Poor   Most of the time people's feelings and motivations are mysteries to me. I definitely need to do better in this area.

❏ **Understanding action plan.** If you rated yourself superior, then you should be sharing your skill by teaching others how to better understand people. If you rated yourself good, fair, or poor, keep striving to learn and improve. You can improve your ability immediately by asking yourself these four questions each time you meet new people:

1. Where did they come from?
2. Where do they want to go?
3. What is their need now?
4. How can I help?

❏ **Activate your positive attitude.** If your ability to understand people isn't as good as you'd like it to be, the root cause may be that you don't value others as highly as you could. As you interact with people, remember the words of Ken Keyes, Jr.: "A loving person lives in a loving world. A hostile person lives in a hostile world: Everyone you meet is your mirror."

CHAPTER 6

A Person of Influence . . .

ENLARGES PEOPLE

MULTIPLY

MENTOR—*Enlarge*

MOTIVATE

MODEL

Once you have been a model of integrity with others and successfully motivated them, you're ready to take the next step in the process of becoming a person of influence in their lives. Jim has a story that will give you an idea of what that next step looks like:

Over the years, Eric has been through more than thirty individual brain operations, but that has never stopped him from being mentally sharp and full of optimism. And his great sense of humor keeps all of us entertained.

During one of his many surgeries, Eric experienced an inter-operative stroke. The resulting loss of muscle balance has limited the use of his right hand and given him severe curvature of the spine. After a couple of years, that required another surgery in which the doctors performed spinal fusion and implanted steel rods from the base of his neck to his pelvis. He spent three months in a full body cast during his long recovery, and as a result, many of his previous abilities were reduced dramatically. But Eric came through it all with characteristically positive spirits.

After Eric's spinal surgery, Nancy could no longer handle him alone, so we decided it was time to employ a full-time home attendant to lift him, help with his daily life, and assist him with his ongoing rehabilitation. We knew the type of person we wanted to hire, but we had no idea where or how to locate him.

One day while Nancy was talking to one of our medical contacts, she heard about a person named Fernando. He sounded great. "He's the perfect person," our friend had said, "but you'll never get him."

Nancy's response was, "Just give us his number, and let us worry about whether or not we can get him."

A few weeks later we hired him, and he has been wonderful. Fernando had been a life skills trainer for Sharp Hospital, and though he was only five years older than Eric, he had already been a manager of a group home for abused kids and had worked in the field of rehab for seven years. He and Eric bonded immediately. Fernando provided a perfect combination of professional skills and companionship.

It's difficult to describe what a wonderful gift God has provided to Eric and our family in the person of Fernando. He sees his mission as that of enlarging Eric, to keep him growing toward his full potential. Fernando constantly learns new information and techniques in his field, and he seeks ways to expose Eric to new experiences and to challenge him to grow. As a result, Eric's life hasn't been the same. In the time that the two of them have been doing things together, Eric has done a lot more than go skiing every year. He has learned to jet ski—I never could have visualized Eric going forty miles per hour on the water, but Fernando believed Eric could do it, and so he did it. Eric also volunteers as a tutor with second graders, studies German, works in our office two days a week, swims a couple of days a week, and has begun to work out with weights. It's hard for us to remember that Eric is severely limited physically, because his life is full, challenging, and expanding every day.

One of Eric's greatest experiences since teaming with Fernando has been his involvement in power soccer. It's a new sport played by people using power wheelchairs. They meet in gymnasiums where they compete as teams and score goals using a large ball. Eric loves it and usually prefers to play goalie.

Not long ago Fernando took Eric to Vancouver, Canada, to compete in a power soccer tournament. It was quite an experience for Eric. They flew together, rented a car, got their hotel room, and got around town—just the two of them. Eric loved it, especially competing in the five-day tournament where he scored two goals. And best of all, his team won the gold medal!

We had never seen Eric so excited as he was when he returned from the tournament. He wore his gold medal home on the plane, and I don't think he touched the ground for days. Since then, his confidence has been so strong that he's willing to tackle just about any kind of challenge. And for that, Fernando deserves a lot of the credit. Without his belief in Eric and his desire to expand his world, none of this would ever have happened.

To become a person of influence and to make a positive impact on people, you have to come alongside them and really get involved in their lives. That's what Fernando did and continues to do with Jim's son Eric. And that's what you need to do with the people for whom you want to make a difference. Modeling a life of integrity is an important first step in becoming an influencer because it creates a strong foundation with others. And the next natural step is motivating people. As you nurture people, show your faith in them, listen to their hopes and fears, and demonstrate your understanding of them, you build a strong relational connection and give them incentive to succeed—and to be influenced by you. But if you want people to be able to *really* grow, improve, and succeed, you have to take the next step with them. You have to become a mentor to them.

THE MEANING OF MENTORING

Giving people the *motivation* to grow without also providing them the *means* of doing it is a tragedy. But the mentoring process offers people the opportunity to turn their potential into reality, their dreams into destiny. Mentors impact eternity because there is no telling where their influence will stop.

Nineteenth-century British statesman William Gladstone asserted, "He is a wise man who wastes no energy on pursuits for which he is not fitted; and he is wiser still who from among the things he can do well, chooses and resolutely follows the best." Most people don't have a natural knack for spotting their greatest areas of potential. They need help doing it, especially as they begin growing and striving to reach their potential. And that's why it's important for you to become a mentor in the lives of the people you desire to help. You need to lead them in their areas of personal and professional growth until they are able to work in these areas more independently.

The authors of *The Leadership Challenge,* James M. Kouzes and Barry Z. Posner, offer insights on leadership that pertain to the subject of mentoring: "Leaders are pioneers. They are people who venture into unexplored territory. They guide us to new and often unfamiliar destinations. . . . The unique reason for having leaders—their differentiating function—is to move us forward. Leaders get us going someplace."

Mentors impact eternity because there is no telling where their influence will stop.

Leading mentors move the people they are developing into growth and areas of strength. In this chapter and in the next three, we'll focus on four ways of accomplishing the task of mentoring others: enlarging people, helping them navigate through life's problems, connecting with them on a deeper level, and empowering them to reach their potential.

Enlarging Others Is an Investment

Author Alan Loy McGinnis observed, "There is no more noble occupation in the world than to assist another human being—to help someone succeed." Helping others enlarge themselves is one of the most incredible things you can ever do for them. As John says in his book *The Success Journey,* growing to reach your potential is one of the three components to being successful (along with knowing your purpose and sowing seeds that benefit others).

Robert Gross, former president of Lockheed Aircraft Corporation, once explained to his supervisors, "It's one thing to build a product; it's another thing to build a company, because companies are nothing but men, and the things that come out of them are no better than the people themselves. We do not build automobiles, airplanes, refrigerators, radios, or shoestrings. We build men. *The men build the product.*"

When you enlarge others, you do several things:

Raise Their Level of Living

Denis Waitley said, "The greatest achievements are those that benefit others." Anytime you help people to enlarge themselves in any area of their lives, you benefit them because you make it possible for them to step up to a new level of living. As people develop their gifts and talents, learn new skills, and broaden their problem-solving abilities, their quality of living and level of contentment improve dramatically. No one can grow and remain unaffected in the way he lives his life.

> *When you enlarge others, you seize*
> *an opportunity to help them*
> *reach their potential.*

Increase Their Potential for Success

Businessman George Crane claimed that "there is no future in any job. The future lies in the man who holds the job." When you enlarge other people, you brighten their future. When they expand their horizons, improve their attitudes, increase their skills, or learn new ways to think, they perform and live better. And that increases their potential.

Increase Their Capacity for Growth

When you help people enlarge themselves, you aren't giving them only a temporary, short-term shot in the arm or tools that will help them only today. Enlarging has long-term benefits. It helps them become better equipped, and it increases their capacity to learn and grow. After being enlarged, whenever they receive a resource or opportunity, they are better able to use it to its greatest benefit. And their growth begins to multiply.

Increase the Potential of Your Organization

If the people you are working to enlarge are a part of a group—no matter whether it is a business, church, sports team, or club—then the whole group benefits from their growth. For example, if many people in your organization improve themselves even slightly, the quality of your whole organization increases. If a few people improve themselves a lot, the potential for growth and success increases due to the increased leadership of these people. And if both kinds of growth occur as the result of your enlarging, hang on because your organization is about to take off!

Fred Smith, a friend of John, is an excellent leader, entrepreneur, and business consultant. Fred had been advising a group of twenty young CEOs and meeting with them monthly for about three years when he decided that they needed to spend some time on their own. So he told them he would not be coming back to see them for a while. They continued to get together without him, but eventually, they asked him to come back for a visit. When he did, they presented him with a piece of Baccarat crystal. On it were etched the words *He stretched us.*

Fred has been stretching and enlarging others for decades because he realizes the incredible value added not only to the people being stretched, but also to all the people they influence. Most people are funny; they want to get ahead and succeed, but they are reluctant to change. They are often willing to grow only enough to accommodate their *problems;* instead, they need to grow enough to achieve their *potential.* That's why they need help from you. Authors Helen Schucman and William Thetford aptly said, "Every situation, properly perceived, becomes an opportunity." When you enlarge others, you seize an opportunity to help them reach their potential.

French essayist Michel Eyquem de Montaigne wrote, "The value of life lies not in the length of days, but in the use we make of them; a man may live long yet live very little." When you enlarge others, you help them make the most of the time they have and raise their quality of life.

Make Yourself an Enlarger

For many people, just because they want to enlarge others doesn't necessarily mean they are ready for the task. They usually need to do some work on themselves first. As in most instances, if you want to do more for others, you have to become more yourself. That's never more valid than in the area of mentoring. You can teach what you know, but you can reproduce only what you are.

Leadership experts Warren Bennis and Bert Nanus spoke to this issue: "It is the capacity to develop and improve their skills that distinguishes leaders from their followers." In your preparations to take on the task of helping others enlarge themselves, the first thing you need to do is improve and enlarge yourself, because only when you are growing and enlarging yourself are you able to help others do the same. Just as people will not follow a person whose leadership skills are weaker than their own, they will not learn to grow from someone who isn't growing. Not only must you be on a higher level in your personal growth, but you must continue to grow on an ongoing basis. (You can probably remember how little you respected one of your high school teachers or college professors who had obviously stopped learning and growing decades earlier—possibly the day he received his degree!)

Albert Schweitzer maintained that "the great secret of success is to go through life as a man who never gets used up." When you make it a goal to continually learn and enlarge yourself, you become the kind of person who can never be "used up." You're always recharging your batteries and finding better ways to get things done. To determine whether you are still growing, ask yourself what you're still looking forward to. If you can't think of anything or you're looking back instead of ahead, your growth may be at a standstill.

It has been said, "The greatest obstacle to discovery is not ignorance. It is the illusion of knowledge." Many people lose sight of the importance of personal growth once they finish their formal education. But don't let that happen to you. Make your growth one of your top priorities starting today. There is no time to waste. As Scottish writer and thinker Thomas

Carlyle put it, "One life; a little gleam of time between two eternities; no second chance for us forever more." Any day that passes without personal growth is an opportunity lost to improve yourself and to enlarge others.

CAREFULLY CHOOSE
PERSONS TO ENLARGE

Once you've done some growing and you're ready to help others enlarge themselves, you need to start thinking about the people you will choose to work with. You have to be selective. You should try to be a model of integrity to all people, whether they're close to you or total strangers. And you should make it your goal to motivate all of the people you have a relationship with—family members, employees, fellow church volunteers, colleagues, and friends. But you can't take the time to enlarge everybody in your life; it's too involved a process. That's why you need to work first with the most promising people around you, the ones most likely to be receptive to growth.

In *Killers of the Dream*, Lillian Smith wrote, "We in America—and men across the earth—have trapped ourselves with that word equality, which is inapplicable to the *genus* man. I wish we would forget it. Stop its use in our country: Let the communists have it. It isn't fit for men who fling their dreams across the skies. It is fit only for a leveling down of mankind." We certainly desire for all people to have equal access to opportunities and justice, but we know that everyone doesn't respond equally to his environment or advantages. And that's true for the people you will have the opportunity to develop. Some people are eager to be enlarged. Others don't care about personal growth or won't grow under your care. It's your job to figure out which is which.

As you think about the people you want to enlarge, keep the following guidelines in mind:

- **Select people whose philosophy of life is similar to yours.** The underlying values and priorities of the people you desire to enlarge need to be similar to yours. If you and they don't have the basics in common, you may end up working at cross-purposes, and you won't experience the effectiveness you would like. Roy Disney, Walt's brother and partner, said, "It's not hard to make decisions when you know what your values are." And if you and the people you mentor have similar values, you will be able to make harmonious decisions as you work together.

- **Choose people with potential you genuinely believe in.** You can't help people you don't believe in. Give your best mentoring effort to people who have the greatest potential—the ones for whom you can see a promising future—not the ones for whom you feel sorry. Nurture, love, and motivate hurting people. But pour yourself into the people who will grow and make a difference.

- **Select people whose lives you can positively impact.** Not everyone you are capable of developing would benefit from what you have to offer. Look for a fit between their potential and your strengths and experience.

- **Match the men and women to the mountains.** We would like all the people we mentor to reach their full potential and develop into stars. After all, the greatest mentors develop people to a level beyond their ability. But the truth is that while all people can move to a higher level than they currently occupy, not everyone is capable of climbing to the highest levels. A successful enlarger evaluates the potential of others and places them in a position to succeed.

- **Start when the time is right.** Start the process at the right time in the lives of others. You've probably heard the expression "strike while the iron is hot." It means to act on a situation at the right time. We've heard that the saying goes back to the fourteenth century. It comes from the practice of blacksmiths who needed to strike metal when it was exactly the right temperature in order to mold it into the precise shape desired. You have to do the same thing with the people you want to enlarge. Start too soon, and they don't yet see the need to grow. Start too late, and you've missed your best opportunity to help them.

Once you've found the right people, keep in mind that you need to get their permission before you start enlarging them. People love to be encouraged and motivated, so you don't need their consent to do either one. But the mentoring process really works only when both parties know the agenda, agree to it, and give it 100 percent effort.

MAKE IT A PRIORITY TO TAKE THEM THROUGH THE ENLARGING PROCESS

Enlarging others can be rewarding and fun, but it also takes time, money, and work. That's why you have to commit yourself to the process and make it a top priority. John's friend Ed Cole says, "There is a price to pay to grow. Commitment is the price." Once you've made the commitment, you're ready to go. The following suggestions will help you maximize the enlarging process:

See Their Potential

Composer Gian Carlo Menotti forcefully stated, "Hell begins on that day when God grants us a clear vision of all that we might have achieved, of all the gifts we wasted, of all that we might have done that we did not do."[1] Unrealized potential is a tragic waste. And as an enlarger, you have the privilege of helping others discover and then develop their potential. But you can't do that until you *see* their potential.

Olympic gold medal swimmer Geoffrey Gaberino sums it up this way: "The real contest is always between what you've done and what you're capable of doing." Whenever you look at people you desire to enlarge, try to discern what they are capable of doing. Look for the spark of greatness. Watch and listen with your heart as well as your eyes. Find their enthusiasm. Try to visualize what they would be doing if they overcame personal obstacles, gained confidence, grew in areas of promise, and gave everything they had. That will help you to see their potential.

Cast a Vision for Their Future

Former presidential speechwriter Robert Orben urged, "Always remember there are only two kinds of people in this world—the realists and the dreamers. The realists know where they're going. The dreamers have already been there." To add value to the people you enlarge, travel ahead of them in your mind's eye and see their future before they do. You become able to cast a vision for their future that helps to motivate and enlarge them.

Someone once said, "Don't let yourself be pressured into thinking that your dreams or your talents aren't prudent. They were never meant to be prudent. They were meant to bring joy and fulfillment into your life." That's great advice. People will never succeed beyond their wildest dreams unless they have some pretty wild dreams. When you cast a vision for others, you help them see their potential and their possibilities. And when you add to that vision your faith in them, you spark them to action. The great British statesman Benjamin Disraeli declared, "Nurture great thoughts for you will never go higher than your thoughts." Help people have great thoughts about themselves, and they will begin to live like the people they can become.

Tap into Their Passion

As an enlarger of people, you are to help people want to grow, and one way to do that is to tap into their passion. Everybody—even the quietest, least demonstrative person—has a passion for something. You just have to find it. As scientist Willis R. Whitney pointed out, "Some men have thousands of reasons why they cannot do what they want to, when all they need is one reason why they can."

As you look for others' passions, go beyond the surface of their daily wants. Look deep within them. Harold Kushner perceptively wrote, "Our souls are not hungry for fame, comfort, wealth, or power. Those rewards create almost as many problems as they solve. Our souls are hungry for meaning, for the sense that we have figured out how to live so that our lives matter, so that the world will at least be a little bit different for our having passed through it."

Once you discover their passion, tap into it. Show them how it can activate their potential to the point that they will be able to realize their vision
for their lives. Passion can help them make their dreams come true. And as
U.S. President Woodrow Wilson said, "We grow by dreams. All big [indi-
viduals] are dreamers. They see things in the soft haze of a spring day, or in
the red fire on a long winter's evening. Some of us let those great dreams
die, but others nourish and protect them; nourish them through bad days
until they bring them to the sunshine and light which comes always to
those who sincerely hope that their dreams will come true." Passion is the
fuel that helps people nourish and protect their dreams.

Address Character Flaws

As you explore how you can help others enlarge themselves, you need
to address any character issues they may have. As we mentioned in
Chapter 1, integrity is the foundation upon which everything else must
stand in people's lives. No matter how much enlarging you do, if the
foundation isn't solid, there's going to be trouble.

When examining the character of others, remember to look beyond
their reputation. Abraham Lincoln made this distinction: "Character is
like a tree and reputation like its shadow. The shadow is what we think of
it; the tree is the real thing." Take time to really get to know the people
you're enlarging. Observe them in various situations. If you get to know
people well enough to know how they react in most situations, you'll have
an idea of where any character shortcomings might be.

Martin Luther King, Jr., said, "The ultimate measure of a man is not
where he stands in moments of comfort and convenience, but where he
stands at times of challenge and controversy." Your goal should be to help
the people you're developing to stand strong in the midst of challenges. But
you have to start with the little things. Author and corporate leader Joseph
Sugarman observed, "Every time you are honest and conduct yourself with
honesty, a success force will drive you toward greater success. Each time
you lie, even with a little white lie, there are strong forces pushing you
toward failure." Help others learn to conduct themselves with integrity in
every situation, and they will be ready to grow and reach their potential.

Focus on Their Strengths

When some people begin to work with others on their development, they often gravitate to weaknesses rather than strengths. Maybe that's because it's so easy to see others' problems and shortcomings. But if you start by putting your energies into correcting people's weaknesses, you will demoralize them and unintentionally sabotage the enlarging process.

We recently heard a baseball story that addresses the subject of people's weaknesses. One afternoon in St. Louis, Stan Musial was having a great game against Chicago pitcher Bobo Newsom. Stan first hit a single, then a triple, and then a home run. When Stan came up to bat for the fourth time, Chicago manager Charlie Grimm decided to yank Bobo and take a chance on a rookie relief pitcher. As the young rookie went to the mound from the bull pen and received the ball from Newsom, he asked, "Say, has this guy Musial got any weaknesses?"

"Yeah," replied Newsom, "he can't hit doubles."

Instead of focusing on weaknesses, pay attention to people's strengths. Sharpen skills that already exist. Compliment positive qualities. Bring out the gifts inherent in them. Weaknesses can wait—unless they are character flaws. Only after you have developed a strong rapport with them and they have begun to grow and gain confidence should you address areas of weakness. And then handle them gently one at a time.

Enlarge Them One Step at a Time

Ronald Osborn noted, "Unless you try to do something beyond what you have already mastered, you will never grow." To enlarge others, help them take growth steps that stretch them regularly without overwhelming or discouraging them.

For each person, that process will look different. But no matter where people are from or where they are going, they need to grow in certain areas. We suggest that you include the following four areas in the development process:

1. Attitude. More than anything else, attitude determines whether people are successful and able to enjoy life. And attitude impacts not only every area of their own lives, but it also influences others.

2. Relationships. The world is made up of people, so everybody has to learn to interact effectively with others. The ability to relate to others and communicate with them can affect marriage, parenting, occupation, friendships, and more. If people can get along, they can get ahead in just about any area of life.

3. Leadership. Everything rises and falls on leadership. If the people you're developing plan to work with others, they have to learn to lead them. If they don't, they'll be carrying the whole load themselves in everything they do.

4. Personal and professional skills. You may be surprised to see that we're listing this last. But the truth is that if thinking isn't positive and skills at working with people are missing, all the professional skills in the world are of little benefit. As you help people grow, work from the inside out. It's not what happens *to* people that makes a difference; it's what happens *in* them.

Put Resources in Their Hands

To help people grow, no matter what area you're addressing, put resources in their hands. Whenever either one of us meets with someone we're developing, we always try to take something with us to give to them—books, tapes, magazine articles, anything uplifting or instructive that we can get our hands on. Nothing gives us greater joy than to know that we've helped someone take another step in growth. That's one reason both of us are constantly creating resources for people's growth. If you can't find exactly what you're looking for to help people, you may want to give from your experience.

The next time you're ready to meet with people whom you want to enlarge, take an active hand in the process. Clip articles written on one of their areas of interest. Give them copies of a book that impacted your life. Or put into their hands tapes that will teach and inspire them. If you keep doing that, not only will the people you develop love the time they spend with you, but each time you meet you'll see that they've grown just a little more toward their potential.

Expose Them to Enlarging Experiences

Implementing a plan for growth enlarges people. But sometimes they need something more to give them a fresh burst of energy and inspiration. Author and champion for the blind Helen Keller said, "One can never consent to creep when one feels an impulse to soar." When you expose people to enlarging experiences, you plant within them that desire to soar.

Conferences and seminars, meetings with outstanding men and women, and special events have made a tremendous impact on us. They always take us out of our comfort zone, move us to think beyond ourselves, or challenge us to go to new levels of living. But remember that events and meetings don't make people grow. They *inspire* people to make important decisions that can change the direction of their lives. The growth itself comes from what people do daily after they have made a decision.

Teach Them to Be Self-Enlargers

According to Philip B. Crosby, "There is a theory of human behavior that says people subconsciously retard their own intellectual growth. They come to rely on clichés and habits. Once they reach the age of their own personal comfort with the world, they stop learning and their mind runs on idle for the rest of their days. They may progress organizationally, they may be ambitious and eager, and they may even work night and day. But they learn no more."

Once you've gotten people to value growth enough to start enlarging themselves, you've broken through a strong barrier. But the next step is to get them to keep growing on their own. It has been said that the goal of all teachers should be to equip students to get along without them. The same can be said of people who seek to enlarge others. As you work with others and help them to enlarge themselves, give them what they need so that they learn to take care of themselves. Teach them to find resources. Encourage them to get out of their comfort zone on their own. And point them toward additional people who can help them learn and grow. If you can help them to become lifelong learners, you will have given them an incredible gift.

> *A successful enlarger evaluates*
> *the potential of others and places them*
> *in a position to succeed.*

We've heard it said, "No one becomes rich unless he enriches another." When you enrich others by helping them grow and enlarge themselves, you not only bring joy to them and yourself, but you also increase your influence and their ability to touch others' lives.

At the beginning of this chapter we told you about how Fernando has enriched the life of Jim and Nancy's son Eric. But there is more to the story:

Since Eric played in that power soccer tournament, he has really changed. He has become more assertive, and he is pursuing his goals with more enthusiasm. For example, Eric has now decided that he wants to try to play tennis, so Fernando has started working with him to get him ready. As I mentioned earlier, Eric has begun weight training. But he has also taken another step to help make tennis possible, a step that at first scared Nancy and me.

Since his stroke, Eric's right hand is extremely limited in what it can do, so he really has full use of only his left hand. But to play tennis, he would have to use his good left hand to hold the racket. What was Fernando's solution? He waited until Nancy and I were out of town and switched Eric's wheelchair controls over to his bad hand. We didn't think it was possible, but it was. Eric now drives right-handed, and as soon as he is ready, he is going to take up tennis.

Eric also does other things that simply astound us. For example, he works in the office, and he puts himself into bed at night. But that's nothing compared to some of his goals: someday Eric wants to be able to drive a car.

Fernando's mentoring and coaching of Eric have been fantastic. We always wanted the best for Eric, but we discovered that we were overly protective. The whole process has enlarged us and broadened our horizons. And of course, it's incredible to see Eric grow and change as he has. But he, Nancy, and I are not alone in that. Even the enlarger has become enlarged. Fernando is changing and growing too. He has always been the consummate professional, but we're now seeing a softer, more loving side that was previously hidden. And recently he told Nancy, "I'm learning that I have to really give to have joy in my life."

What nineteenth-century American philosopher-poet Ralph Waldo Emerson said is true: "It is one of the most beautiful compensations of this life that no man can sincerely try to help another without helping himself." If you give yourself to enlarging others and assisting them in reaching their potential, the rewards you reap will be almost as great as the ones of the people you help.

Influence Checklist

ENLARGING PEOPLE

❑ **Whom will you enlarge?** Write down the names of the top three candidates for you to enlarge. Remember to pick people whose philosophy of life is similar to yours, whose potential you believe in, whose lives you can positively impact, and who are ready for the process.

1. _____

2. _____

3. _____

❑ **Enlargement agenda.** Use the following grid to develop your strategy for enlarging the three persons you selected:

	Person 1	Person 2	Person 3
Name	_____	_____	_____
Potential	_____	_____	_____
Passion	_____	_____	_____
Character Issue(s)	_____	_____	_____
Greatest Strength	_____	_____	_____
Next Step in Development	_____	_____	_____
Resource for Current Need	_____	_____	_____
Next Enlarging Experience	_____	_____	_____

CHAPTER 7

A Person of Influence . . .

NAVIGATES FOR OTHER PEOPLE

MULTIPLY

MENTOR—*Navigate*

MOTIVATE

MODEL

Helping people enlarge themselves and develop their potential makes it possible for them to go to a whole new level of living. But no matter how much they grow and learn, they will still face obstacles. They will make mistakes. They will run into problems in their personal and professional lives. And they will encounter circumstances that they won't be able to get through well without some help.

John tells a story about a time when he decided to help a whole planeload of people get through a tough day together:

I travel a lot because of the speaking I do around the country, and sometimes that leads to unusual situations. I remember one particular evening when I was in the airport in Charlotte, North Carolina, getting ready to fly to Indianapolis, Indiana. I was on the phone up to the last minute, and then I dashed up to my gate and met Dick Peterson, the president of INJOY, expecting to run onto the plane just before the doors closed. But to my surprise, the waiting area had about fifty or sixty people moping around in it.

I looked at Dick and said, "What's going on?"

"Well," said Dick, "it looks like we won't get to fly out for a while yet."

"What's the problem?" I asked.

"I don't know," he said.

So I went up and talked to the agent at the gate, and he told me, "The flight attendants aren't here yet, and we can't allow anyone to board until they come." Then he announced the same thing over the PA system, and I could see everyone in the waiting area kind of deflate. They looked miserable.

I looked at Dick, and I said, "You know, let's see if we can help these people out." So we went to a snack counter close by, and I told the woman there, named Denise, "I'd like sixty Coca-Colas, please."

She stared at me a moment and finally said, "You want sixty?"

Then I explained to her, "There are a whole bunch of passengers down at that next gate who are disappointed, and they need something to boost their morale."

"You're not kidding? You're going to buy one for everybody?" she asked.

"You bet."

She paused for a moment, then said, "Can I help?"

She, Dick, and I took those drinks down to the people at the gate, and I could see that they weren't sure what to think. So I said, "May I have your attention, please? My name is John Maxwell. Since we're not going to leave for thirty to forty-five minutes, I thought I would at least get you something to drink. It's on the house."

We started passing out the Cokes, and I could tell they thought I was weird. So did the airline personnel. But after a while I began to develop rapport with them, and when they found out the flight attendants were on the ground and would be at the gate soon, I was finally able to talk them into letting us get on the plane.

As soon as we all got on the plane, I saw a large basket of peanuts, granola bars, and goodies in the galley, and I thought to myself, *Hey, they ought to have something to eat with that Coca-Cola.* So I went down the aisle giving out the goodies. In only five minutes I had served them all something to eat, and they were drinking their Cokes. About this time the flight crew rushed aboard. They were very apologetic. They got on the plane's PA system right away and said, "Ladies and gentlemen, we're going to get started right away. As soon as we can, we'll begin the beverage service."

Well, they could hear a lot of laughter and chattering in the cabin, and one of the flight attendants said to the other, "What's going on here?"

"Hi, my name's John," I said. "They're not too worried about your service right now. I've already given everybody something to drink and some snacks to eat. In fact, would it be all right if I talked to everybody a moment?" They laughed and said, "Sure. Why not?"

As we taxied out to the runway, they let me talk. "Hi, folks," I said, "this is your friend, John Maxwell. Please buckle up. We'll be airborne in a few moments, and as soon as we're in the air, I'll be back again to serve you."

We had a great time on that flight. I talked to everybody and helped serve drinks. When we landed, I asked if I could talk to everybody one last time. "Gang," I said, "this is John. I'm so glad you were on this flight today. Didn't we have a wonderful time?" Everyone clapped and cheered. "Now when we get off, I'm going to go down to the baggage claim area. If any of you have any problems, please see me, and we'll immediately take care of the situation."

While I was down in the baggage area helping people find their luggage, a man came up to me and said, "This has been great. I'm from Florida, and I've got some grapefruit with me. Here, have a grapefruit."

"Thank you very much," I said. "You know, I've got a brother who lives in Florida—in Winterhaven."

"That's where I live!" he said. "What's your name again? John Maxwell? Wait! Is your brother's name Larry and his wife, Anita?"

"That's correct."

"I know them!" he said. "Anita serves on a board with me. I'm going to call them right now. They won't believe it." He hurried off toward a bank of phones. "I've traveled for years," he said, "and nothing like this has ever happened before!"

What could have been a miserable plane ride of tired, grumpy people turned out to be an experience that nobody on that flight will ever forget. Why? Because one person decided to take others under his wing and help them through a potentially unpleasant situation. It's a process that we call *navigating*.

Most people need help working through some of life's difficulties. That plane flight probably wasn't more than an inconvenience for most of those passengers, but they still enjoyed being coached through the experience by someone with a good attitude. That kind of assistance is needed and appreciated by most people, especially when life's complicated problems hit closer to home, and people have a tougher time with them.

A person well known for trying to help people work through their problems is Ann Landers. Talking about what she has learned from people through the letters she has received for her column, Ann Landers said:

I've learned plenty—including, most meaningfully, what Leo Rosten had in mind when he said, "Each of us is a little lonely, deep inside, and cries to be understood." I have learned how it is with the stumbling, tortured people in this world who have nobody to talk to. The fact that the column has been a success underscores, for me at least, the central tragedy of our society, the disconnectedness, the insecurity, the fear that bedevils, cripples, and paralyzes so many of us. I have learned that financial success, academic achievement, and social or political status open no doors to peace of mind or inner security. We are all wanderers, like sheep, on this planet.[1]

The people in your life with whom you have influence need your help, especially the ones who are trying to go to a new level, start a new venture, or enter a new phase of life. They need someone to lead and guide them. Mel Ziegler, founder of Banana Republic, outlined a leader's ability to navigate when he wrote: "A leader discovers the hidden chasm between where things are and where things would better be, and strings up a makeshift bridge to attempt the crossing. From the other side he guides those who dare to cross his rickety traverse until the engineers can build a sturdier span for all."[2]

> *A leader is one who sees more*
> *than others see, who sees farther than others*
> *see, and who sees before others do.*
> —*Leroy Eims*

Ziegler painted a vivid picture. But for most people, the leadership they need isn't just a one-time event, a single chasm to cross. Most people need guidance on a fairly continual basis until they can get their lives together, and then they can be encouraged to make the trip under their own power. It's more like an ocean voyage that you have to navigate them through than a chasm you have to coax them to cross. You've got to help them find their way, spot icebergs, and weather stormy seas, and you've got to take the trip with them—at least until they are on the right course and can learn to navigate on their own.

A NAVIGATOR IDENTIFIES
THE DESTINATION

A good navigator helps people identify their destination. In *Be the Leader You Were Meant to Be,* Leroy Eims wrote, "A leader is one who sees more than others see, who sees farther than others see, and who sees before others do." In the previous chapter, we talked about the importance of casting a vision of people's future so that they are encouraged to grow. The next step is to show them their destination in a more concrete way. Most people who are dissatisfied and discouraged feel that way because they haven't grabbed hold of a vision for themselves. It has been said, "To bury our dreams is to bury ourselves, for we are really 'such stuff as dreams are made on.' God's dream for us is to reach our potential." You have to help others discover their dream and then get them moving toward it. If there is no movement, then there can be no navigation. And any movement will be progress only if it's in the direction of the destination.

You may already recognize much of the potential of the people you're trying to mentor, but you need to know more about them. To help them recognize the destination they will be striving for, you need to know what really matters to them, what makes them tick. To do that, find out these things:

- **What do they cry about?** To know where people truly want to go, you need to know what touches their hearts. Passion and compassion are compelling motivators. It has been said that the great men and women of history were great not for what they owned or earned, but for what they gave their lives to accomplish. Listen with your heart and you are likely to discover the things for which others are willing to give themselves.
- **What do they sing about?** Frank Irving Fletcher observed, "No man can deliver the goods if his heart is heavier than his load." There is a big difference between the things that touch people's hearts and the things that weigh them down. In the long run, people need to

focus a lot of energy on what gives them joy. Looking for enthusi-
asms in the people you mentor will give you another clue concerning their intended destination.

- **What do they dream about?** Napoleon Hill said, "Cherish your
  visions and your dreams as they are the children of your soul; the
  blueprints of your ultimate achievements." If you can help people
  discover their dreams and truly believe in them, you can help them
  become the persons they were designed to be.

A Navigator Plots the Course

When you consider people's passions, potential, and vision, you are
better able to see where they really want to go, because you view them
with more depth and discernment. Often, people say that their goal is
happiness or success, but if they identify such a surface thing as their destination, they're sure to be disappointed. As John Condry emphasized,
"Happiness, wealth, and success are by-products of goal-setting; they cannot be the goal themselves."

Once you as the navigator assist others in identifying a vision for
their lives, you need to help them find a way to make it a reality. And
that means plotting a course and setting goals. J. Meyers said, "A #2
pencil and a dream can take you anywhere." No doubt he understood
the value of planning and putting goals in writing. That doesn't mean
that things always go as you expect, but you have to start with a game
plan. A good rule of thumb is to set your goals in concrete and write
your plans in sand.

To help people plot their course, give attention to these areas:

Where They Need to Go

You would be amazed by how far off track some people can get when
trying to reach their goals. As E. W. Howe wrote in *Success Is Easier Than
Failure,* "Some people storm imaginary Alps all their lives, and die in the
foothills cursing difficulties that do not exist." People who have not yet

experienced success often have no idea what it takes to get from where they are to where they want to go. They throw themselves into a labyrinth of activity because they don't recognize that they can take an easier path. As the navigator, you are to show them the best course.

What They Need to Know

We heard an amusing story about a husband who wanted to help his wife because he suspected she had a hearing problem. One night he positioned himself across the room from her with her back to him, and softly he said, "Can you hear me?" He didn't get an answer from her, so he moved closer and repeated, "Can you hear me now?" Still nothing. He moved closer and asked, "Can you hear me?" He heard no response, so finally he repeated the question from directly behind her. She turned to face him and said, "For the fourth time, *Yes!*"

Too many people out there are similar to that husband. They want to succeed and help others, but their misunderstanding or lack of knowledge hinders them. A good navigator recognizes the blind spots in others, gently identifies them, and helps people overcome them.

How They Need to Grow

When you are navigating for others, remember that they can't make the whole trip in a day. They have to grow into their goals and take things one step at a time. An experiment performed by Alfred J. Marrow, a company president with a Ph.D. in psychology, illustrated this fact. He was interested in finding a way to help new unskilled employees reach optimum performance and match the standards of his skilled, experienced employees as quickly as possible.

Marrow decided to divide some new employees into two groups. With the first, he asked the unskilled workers to match the production of the skilled ones by the end of twelve weeks. With the second group, he established escalating weekly goals. Each week's goal was slightly more ambitious than the one from the week before.

A #2 pencil and a dream
can take you anywhere.
—J. Meyers

In the first group with the single goal, only 66 percent of the workers were able to meet his expectations. But the second group with the intermediate goals performed significantly better and was able to match the production averages of the company's experienced laborers more quickly.[3]

As you work with people, help them to figure out not only their long-term destination, but also the smaller steps along the way. Help them identify attainable goals that will give them confidence, and they'll make progress.

A NAVIGATOR THINKS AHEAD

Few things are more discouraging than being blindsided, especially when someone who could have helped you stands by and watches it happen. That's why thinking ahead for others is part of your task as a navigator. As people's leader and mentor, you have been places they have not yet gone, had experiences they have not been through, and gained insights they have not yet developed. You have the ability to prepare them for what they are going to face. If you don't, you're not helping them the way you should, and you are no longer performing one of your most important functions as a leader. American humorist Arnold H. Glasow saw the significance of this: "One of the tests of leadership is to recognize a problem before it becomes an emergency." That's something the less-experienced persons you're helping cannot at first do on their own.

Here are four things you should help them understand as they get under way:

1.   Everybody Faces Problems

Someone quipped, "If you keep your head when all about you are losing theirs, you just don't understand the problem." As you mentor people and help them grow, you may find that they expect to someday reach a point in their lives when their problems disappear. But they need to realize that everybody has problems. No matter how far they go or how successful they become, they will continue to face difficulties. Or as writer and artists' advocate Elbert Hubbard said, "The man who has no more problems to solve is out of the game."

The Barna Research Group surveyed more than twelve hundred people to gather information on the problems they faced. They were asked to identify their single most serious need or problem. Here are their answers along with the percentage of people who ranked the problems most pressing:

> 39%   Financial
> 16%   Job-Related
> 12%   Personal Health
> 8%   Time and Stress
> 7%   Parenting
> 6%   Educational Attainment
> 3%   Fear of Crime
> 3%   Personal Relationships[4]

As you can see, people face a variety of problems, with money being the greatest. Be prepared to give them assistance. And remember to settle your own issues before trying to help others with theirs.

2.   Successful People Face More Problems Than Unsuccessful People

Another common misconception is that successful people have achieved because they didn't have problems. But that isn't true. In his book *Holy Sweat,* Tim Hansel tells this story:

In 1962, Victor and Mildred Goertzel published a revealing study of 413 famous and exceptionally gifted people. The study was called *Cradles of Eminence.* These two researchers spent years trying to understand the source of these people's greatness, the common thread which ran through all of these outstanding people's lives. The most outstanding fact was that almost all of them, 392, had to overcome very difficult obstacles in order to become who they were. Their problems became opportunities instead of obstacles.[5]

Not only do people overcome obstacles to become successful, but even after they have achieved a level of success, they continue to face problems. The bad news is that the higher people go—personally and professionally—the more complicated life gets. Schedules get tighter, money issues increase, and greater demands are put on successful people. But the good news is that if they continue to grow and develop themselves, their ability to deal with problems will also increase.

3. *Money Doesn't Solve Problems*

Another faulty belief is that money solves all problems. The opposite is actually true—people with money tend to be less content and have additional problems. For example, Ernie J. Zelinski cites a recent survey showing that a higher percentage of people making more than $75,000 a year are dissatisfied with their incomes than of those making less than $75,000 a year. He also noted:

A larger percentage of the rich have alcohol and drug problems than the general population. I have a theory about how well off we will be with a lot of money. If we are happy and handle problems well when we are making $25,000 a year, we will be happy and handle problems well when we have a lot more money. If we are unhappy and don't handle problems well on $25,000 a year, we can expect the same of ourselves with a lot of money. We will be just as unhappy and handle problems as ineffectively, but with more comfort and style.[6]

The bottom line is that you should try to help people understand that money is no substitute for the basic problem-solving skills they need to develop. Financial problems are usually a symptom of other personal problems.

4. Problems Provide an Opportunity for Growth

As you look ahead and help people, realize that while problems can cause pain, they also provide an excellent opportunity for growth. Or as author Nena O'Neill put it, "Out of every crisis comes the chance to be reborn."

The people of Enterprise, Alabama, understand that idea. In their town stands a monument to the Mexican boll weevil, erected in 1919. The story behind it is that in 1895, the insect destroyed the county's major crop, cotton. After that disaster, local farmers began to diversify, and the peanut crop of 1919 far exceeded the value of even the best ones comprised of cotton. On the monument are the following words: "In profound appreciation of the boll weevil and what it has done as the herald of prosperity. . . . Out of a time of struggle and crisis has come new growth and success. Out of adversity has come blessing."

As you have certainly observed, not everyone approaches life's problems in the same way. Historian Arnold Toynbee believed that all people react in one of four ways under difficult circumstances:

1. Retreat into the past
2. Daydream about the future
3. Retreat within and wait for someone to rescue them
4. Face the crisis and transform it into something useful

As you help others, let them know there may be rough waters ahead. Show them that it's wise to plan ahead as best they can. And when trouble comes, encourage them to face it and try to become better as a result.

A Navigator Makes
Course Corrections

We've heard that back before the time of sophisticated electronic navigational equipment, the ship's navigator used to take a reading of the stars at a particular time in the middle of the night, determine how far off course the vessel was, and make adjustments to its course. No matter how accurately the original course had been laid out or how carefully the helmsman had followed his orders, the ship always got off course and needed adjustments.

People are the same way. No matter how focused they are or how well they plan, people will still get off course. The problem comes when they have difficulty making course corrections—either because they don't know they're off course, or because they don't know what they should do to fix things. Not everyone is a natural problem solver. For most people, it's a skill they must learn. John Foster Dulles, secretary of state during the Eisenhower administration, proposed that "the measure of success is not whether you have a tough problem to deal with, but whether it's the same problem you had last year." As the navigator, you can help people avoid that situation.

Teach Them Not to Listen to
Doubting Critics

In the book *Principle-Centered Leadership,* Stephen Covey tells how Columbus was once invited to a banquet where he was given the most honored place at the table. A shallow courtier who was jealous of him asked abruptly, "Had you not discovered the Indies, are there not other men in Spain who would have been capable of the enterprise?"

Columbus made no reply but took an egg and invited the company to make it stand on end. They all attempted to do it, but none succeeded, whereupon the explorer tapped it on the table, denting one end, and left it standing.

"We all could have done it that way!" the courtier cried.

"Yes, if you had only known how," answered Columbus. "And once I showed you the way to the New World, nothing was easier than to follow it."

When you are navigating for others,
remember that they can't
make the whole trip in a day.

The truth is that it's a hundred times easier to criticize others than to find solutions to problems. But criticism gets you nowhere. Alfred Armand Montapert summed it up this way: "The majority see the obstacles; the few see the objectives; history records the successes of the latter, while oblivion is the reward of the former." Help the people within your influence to ignore the critics and keep their eyes on the big picture. Show them that the best way to silence critics is to solve the problem and move on.

Coach Them Not to Be Overwhelmed by Challenges

A rookie major-league baseball player faced pitcher Walter Johnson for the first time when Johnson was in his prime. The batter took two quick strikes and headed for the dugout. He told the umpire to keep the third strike—he had seen enough.

When faced with tough problems, just about anybody is likely to get discouraged. That's why it's a good idea to coach people through their problems, especially early on in the mentoring process while you're first helping them to navigate. Encourage them to maintain a positive attitude, and give them strategies for problem solving.

Management expert Ken Blanchard recommends a four-step problem-solving process that includes (1) thinking about the problem in order to make it specific, (2) forming theories for solving it, (3) forecasting the consequences of carrying out the theories, and (4) then choosing which method to use based on the big picture. Blanchard says, "Whether you choose a vacation or a spouse, a party or a candidate, a cause to contribute to or a creed to live by—think!" There are no impossible problems. Time, thought, and a positive attitude can solve just about anything.

Encourage Them to Seek Simple Solutions

There are a couple of keys to the most effective method of problem solving. The first is recognizing that the simple way to solve a problem is better than the most clever one. An example from the life of Thomas Edison illustrates this point well. It's said that Edison had a unique way of hiring engineers. He would give the applicant a lightbulb and ask, "How much water will it hold?" There were two ways the engineers usually went about solving the problem. The first way was to use gauges to measure all the angles of the bulb, and then use those figures to calculate the surface area. That approach sometimes took as long as twenty minutes. The second way was to fill the bulb with water and then pour the contents into a measuring cup, which usually took about one minute.[7] Edison never hired the engineers who used the first method. He didn't want the engineers to impress him—he wanted them to provide simple results.

The second element in effective problem solving is the ability to make decisions. Thomas J. Watson, Jr., former head of IBM, believed that solving problems quickly was essential to making progress. "Solve it," he declared. "Solve it quickly, solve it right or wrong. If you solve it wrong, it will come back and slap you in the face, and then you can solve it right. Lying dead in the water and doing nothing is a comfortable alternative because it is without risk, but it is an absolutely fatal way to manage a business." And it's also a terrible way for people to manage their lives. Help others to realize when they need to make course adjustments, find simple solutions that they think will work, and then execute them without delay. Don't let them continue traveling off course for any length of time.

Instill Confidence in Them

One pitfall of helping others with their problems and mistakes is that they can doubt themselves. Continually encourage the people you help. George Matthew Adams said, "What you think means more than anything else in your life. More than what you earn, more than where you live, more than your social position, and more than what anyone else may think about you." The size of the persons and the quality of their attitude are more important than the size of any problem they may face. If your people remain confident, they will be able to overcome any obstacle.

A Navigator Stays with the People

Finally, a good navigator takes the trip with the people he is guiding. He doesn't give directions and then walk away. He travels alongside his people as a friend. Author and conference speaker Richard Exley explained his idea of friendship this way: "A true friend is one who hears and understands when you share your deepest feelings. He supports you when you are struggling; he corrects you, gently and with love, when you err; and he forgives you when you fail. A true friend prods you to personal growth, stretches you to your full potential. And most amazing of all, he celebrates your successes as if they were his own."

As you come alongside some of the people within your influence and mentor them, you and they may experience difficult times together. You won't be perfect and neither will they, but just keep in mind Henry Ford's words: "Your best friend is he who brings out the best that is within you." Do your best to follow that objective, and you will help a lot of people.

Once people learn to become effective problem solvers and can navigate for themselves, their lives begin to change dramatically. No longer do they feel powerless in the face of life's difficult circumstances. They learn to roll with the punches—and even to duck a few. And once problem solving becomes a habit, no challenge seems too large.

Jim is an excellent thinker and problem solver. He has navigated through some pretty interesting situations over the years. Recently, he recounted a story that you will undoubtedly enjoy:

> A couple of years ago while Nancy and I were hosting a business seminar aboard a large cruise ship in the Caribbean, we were called away to an important business meeting in Michigan. We had no problem get-

ting to the meeting because arrangements had been made for us to be picked up by a private jet at the airport in San Juan, Puerto Rico. But leaving Michigan and getting back turned out to be quite another story.

Our plan was to return on the same jet the next day and meet the ship at its next port. From there the ship would return to Miami, and we could continue teaching our seminar. But in Michigan when we began to depart, our aircraft developed a problem and had to return to the hangar. That caused a serious problem for us. There were no commercial flights to our destination, nor were there any private planes with enough range to get us down to St. Martin, which is some fifteen hundred miles off the coast of Florida.

Missing the seminar simply was not an option for us, so we looked at other possibilities. The best we could do was take an available private jet to Atlanta and work on finding another plane to take us the rest of the way.

By the time we touched down in Atlanta, we had managed to arrange for another plane, and it was ready and waiting for us. As soon as our plane came to a stop, we gathered up our things and scrambled over to the other jet. You can imagine how relieved we were to get on board and get in the air.

We weren't on our way for very long before we found out that our current flight was going to get us on the island exactly fifteen minutes after the ship was scheduled to depart. "We've got to get them to delay the ship," I said.

The pilot started working on the problem via radio and managed to contact the ship's captain from the cockpit. He agreed to a twenty-minute delay. Then the pilot worked on getting us a quick clearance through customs. And when word came back that we would be able to do it, we started getting optimistic.

We dashed to the first taxi we could find and headed out, but almost immediately, we hit a huge traffic jam.

"How far is it to the ship?" Nancy asked.

"On the other side of the island," the driver answered.

"How long will that take?'

"Fifteen, maybe twenty minutes."

"We need to make it in less than ten," I said, offering him a really good tip.

He looked at me, looked at the money, and said, "Yes, sir." He pulled the cab over onto the sidewalk and made a quick turn up an alley. We went over curbs, through lights, and weaved down alleys and side streets in a blur. We felt as if we were on Mr. Toad's Wild Ride at Disneyland. It seemed like we saw the back of every building on the island. But then we shot through a narrow opening between two buildings and careened out into the sunlight onto a pier—and the ship was in sight, its horn sounding its imminent departure.

As we screeched to a halt at the end of the pier, we piled out of the cab. That's when we began to hear the cheering. Evidently, word had gotten to our people on the ship that we were fighting to make our way back to them. And when we finally had a second to look up, we could see more than five hundred people on deck whooping and clapping and cheering to celebrate our arrival.

"Who are you, anyway?" our driver asked. I just handed him the money and said, "Thanks for your help." Then Nancy and I ran for the gangway. It hadn't been easy, but we had made it.

The ability to navigate problems and overcome obstacles is a skill that anyone can learn, but it takes practice. If Jim and Nancy had faced that same situation twenty years before, they probably would not have made it to that ship. But over the years, they've developed an incredible ability to make things happen, not only in their own lives, but also in the lives of others.

You can have that same ability. Become a navigator in the lives of others. You will be able to use your influence to help them move up to the next level in their lives, and if you assist them during their darkest hours, you will make friends of them for life.

<u>Influence Checklist</u>
NAVIGATING FOR OTHER PEOPLE

❏ **Identify their destination.** Think about the three people you've decided to enlarge. What are their destinations? Observe what makes them cry, sing, and dream. Write those things down here:

Person 1: _____

Cry: _____

Sing: _____

Dream: _____

Person 2: _____

Cry: _____

Sing: _____

Dream: _____

Person 3: _____

Cry: _____

Sing: _____

Dream: _____

❏ **Look ahead.** Based on your experience and knowledge of these people, list the difficulties you think they are likely to face in the near future:

1. _____
2. _____
3. _____

❏ **Plan ahead.** How can you help them navigate through these potential problems? Write down what you can do and when you should do it.

1. _____
2. _____
3. _____

CHAPTER 8

A Person of Influence . . .

CONNECTS
WITH PEOPLE

MULTIPLY

MENTOR—*Connect*

MOTIVATE

MODEL

Have you ever been to a family or school reunion? It can be fun because it gives you a chance to connect with people you haven't seen in a long time. John recently went to a reunion of sorts, and he had an incredible time. Let him tell you about it:

My first job out of college in 1969 was at a little church in Hillham, Indiana. I was the senior pastor there for three years. The church really grew during the short time Margaret and I were there, so much so that we had to construct a new church building in 1971 to hold all the people. We look back on those three years as a crucial growing time in our lives that we really enjoyed and benefited from.

Recently, I got a phone call from that little country church. The person on the phone excitedly explained they were getting ready to celebrate the twenty-five-year anniversary of the building we constructed. They were preparing to have a big service and invite everybody for miles around to come celebrate with them. And then the person on the other end of the phone paused and cleared his throat. And he finally asked, "Dr. Maxwell, would you be willing to come back and preach that Sunday service for us?"

"I would love to come back and preach at your service," I told him. "It would be an honor. You just tell me the day, and I'll be there."

During the next few months, I spent some time thinking about how I could make their anniversary a great day for them. The last thing I wanted to do was come back as some kind of conquering hero. I knew I needed to find ways to connect with them.

The first thing I did was get them to send me a copy of their church directory with the pictures and names of all the people in their congregation. There in the book were many faces I recognized. Some people had less hair than I remembered, and much of that hair was now gray, but I knew the faces behind those twenty-five years of wrinkles. And there were many others who were new to me. Sons and daughters of the people I loved, and some new names I didn't recognize. I spent many hours poring over those pictures and memorizing those names.

Then I prepared the best message I could, one filled with stories of our common experiences. I shared some of my mistakes and recounted all of their victories. I wanted them to know that they shared in my success. They were king makers, and I felt very privileged to have served them for three years and benefited from their loving support and care for me.

But I knew that more important than the message I preached or anything else I could do would be the time I was able to spend with the people. So when the time came, Margaret and I flew in early, and we spent Saturday afternoon with some of the old-timers who had been such a vital part of our ministry twenty-five years before. We shared a lot of wonderful recollections. I talked to them about some of my fondest memories, and they surprised me with a few stories of their own. For instance, there was one man in a wheelchair who had been a teenager when I was the pastor there. He had been in an accident that left him in a coma. I had visited him and his family several times in the hospital, and one night I shared my faith with him as he lay unconscious in his bed. I left Hillham soon after that to go to my next church, and until my current visit, I hadn't known he had ever awakened from the coma.

"Do you remember coming into the hospital and talking to me twenty-five years ago?" he asked.

"I sure do," I answered.

"So do I," he told me. "I remember that day as clear as can be. I wasn't able to answer you, but I heard every word you said. That's the day I became a believer." And he told me about how his faith had impacted other people in the community. It was a very special time.

The next day, I got to the church early to shake the hands of the people as they came into the sanctuary. It was wonderful to get to meet so many of the people and be able to greet them by name. And I preached a message of affirmation to them. Even though they had done some wonderful things since I had last seen them, I told them that I could see that in the next twenty-five years lay their greatest potential. Their best days were still ahead of them. And when I left, I felt as though I had not only renewed some old acquaintances, but also had made a lot of new friends.

The time John spent with the people in Hillham was brief, but in that short time, he was able to do something that was important to them and him. He was able to connect with them.

CONNECTING ENABLES OTHERS TO TRAVEL TO A HIGHER LEVEL

Connection is a very important part of the process of mentoring others. And it's absolutely critical if you want to influence people in a positive way. When you navigate for others, you come alongside them and travel their road for a while, helping them handle some of the obstacles and difficulties in their lives. But when you connect with them, you are asking them to come alongside you and travel your road for your and their mutual benefit.

When we think of connecting with people, we compare it to trains and what happens to them in a train yard. The cars sitting on the tracks in a train yard have a lot of things going for them. They have value because they're loaded with cargo; they have a destination; and they even have a route by which to get to that destination. But they don't have a way of getting anywhere on their own. To do anything of value, they have to hook up with a locomotive.

Have you ever been to a train yard and watched how unrelated and disconnected pieces of equipment come together to form a working train? It's quite a process. It all begins with the locomotive. First, it switches itself onto the same track as the car it's going to pick up. Then it moves to where the car is, backs up to it, makes contact with it, and connects. Once it's all hooked up, together they move toward their destination.

A similar thing must happen before you can get people to go with you on a journey. You have to find out where they are, move toward them to make contact, and connect with them. If you can do that successfully, you can take them to new heights in your relationship and in their development. Remember, the road to the next level is always uphill, and people need help to make it to that higher level.

NINE STEPS FOR CONNECTING
WITH PEOPLE

Fortunately, you don't have to be an engineer to connect with people, but it does take effort to make connection happen. You'll need communication skills, a desire to help people grow and change, and a sense of personal mission or purpose—after all, you have to know where you're going to take others along.

Take a look at the following steps, and use them to help you connect with the people you influence:

1. Don't Take People for Granted

You can connect with people and lead them only if you value them. Weak leaders sometimes get so caught up in the vision of where they're going that they forget the people they're trying to lead. But you can't take people for granted for any length of time before your leadership begins to fall apart. And you won't be able to connect with them.

A wonderful story from former Speaker of the House Tip O'Neill reveals what can happen when you take people for granted. He said that on one election day, an elderly neighbor came up to him after leaving the polls and said, "Tip, I voted for you today even though you didn't ask me."

O'Neill was surprised. "Mrs. O'Brien," he said, "I've known you all my life. I took your garbage out for you, mowed your lawn, shoveled snow for you. I didn't think I had to ask."

"Tip," she said in a motherly tone, "it's always *nice* to be asked." O'Neill said he never forgot that piece of advice.

Valuing people is the first step in the connection process, but it has additional benefits. When you let people know that you don't take them for granted, they turn around and do the same for you. John was reminded of this by his friend and colleague Dan Reiland. John will tell you the story:

Margaret and I spent a long weekend with Dan and his wife, Patti, not too long ago. Dan has worked with me for fifteen years, first as my executive pastor at Skyline Church where I was the senior pastor, and now as a vice president at INJOY. We spent the weekend at a resort hotel in Laguna Beach. It was great. We enjoyed the pool and spa, ate some great meals, and had a wonderful time together.

As Margaret and I were checking out, I went to the front desk to pay the bill and discovered that Dan had beaten me there and already taken care of everything. Later I talked to him and said, "Dan, you didn't have to do that. I wanted to treat you and Patti."

"No, John," said Dan, "it was our pleasure. You do so much for us; I never want to take you for granted."

John's friend Coach Bill McCartney, former head football coach of the Colorado State Buffaloes, said, "Anytime you devalue people, you question God's creation of them." You can never tell people too often, too loudly, or too publicly how much you love them.

> *You can connect with people*
> *and lead them only if you value them.*

2.   Possess a Make-a-Difference Mind-Set

If you desire to accomplish something great and really want to see it happen, you need to possess a make-a-difference attitude. Anytime you don't believe you can make a difference, you won't. How do you cultivate a solid make-a-difference mind-set?

Believe you can make a difference. Every person on this earth—including you—has the potential to make a difference. But you can do it only if you believe in yourself and are willing to give yourself away to others. As Helen Keller said, "Life is an exciting business and most exciting when lived for others." You may not be able to help *everybody*, but you can certainly help *somebody*.

Believe what you share can make a difference. The two of us spend a large part of our lives connecting and communicating with people. Between the two of us, we impact more than one million people every year. If we believed that what we share with others couldn't make a difference, we would quit tomorrow. But we know that we can help others change their lives. We believe that everything rises and falls on leadership. We're certain that people's attitudes make or break them. And we know that there is no joy, peace, or meaning in life without faith.

You have to believe that what you have to offer others can make a difference in their lives. No one wants to follow a person without conviction. If you don't believe, neither will other people.

Believe the person you share with can make a difference. We've read about something called a reciprocity rule in human behavior. It states that over time, people come to share similar attitudes toward one another. In other words, if we hold a high opinion of you and continue to hold that opinion, eventually, you will come to feel the same way about us. That process builds a connection between us, and it opens the way for a powerful partnership.

Believe that together you can make a big difference. Mother Teresa is a good example of a truth she once expressed: "I can do what you can't do, and you can do what I can't do. *Together* we can do great things." No one ever achieves alone what he can do when partnering with others. And anybody who doesn't recognize that falls incredibly short of her potential.

There is a story about a famous organist in the 1800s that illustrates the importance of recognizing valuable partnerships. The musician traveled from town to town giving concerts. In each town, he hired a boy to pump the organ during the concert. After one particular performance, he couldn't shake the boy. He even followed the organist back to his hotel.

"We sure had us a great concert tonight, didn't we?" said the boy.

"What do you mean *we*?" said the musician. "*I* had a great concert. Now why don't you go home?"

The next night when the organist was halfway through a magnificent fugue, the organ suddenly quit. The organist was stupefied. Then suddenly, the little boy stuck his head around the corner of the organ, grinned, and said, "We ain't having a very good concert tonight, are *we*?"

If you want to connect with people and take them with you to a higher level, recognize the difference you can make as a team, and acknowledge it at every opportunity.

3. Initiate Movement Toward Them

According to Tom Peters and Nancy Austin, "The number one managerial productivity problem in America is, quite simply, managers who are out of touch with their people and out of touch with their customers."[1] Lack of contact and communication is a problem that affects many people, not just managers in organizations. Maybe that's why sales expert Charles B. Ruth says, "There are many cases of salesmen who have nothing to offer a prospect except friendship out-selling salesmen with everything to offer—except friendship."[2]

We believe there are many reasons why people don't connect with one another more than they do. A primary reason, especially within organizations, is that many leaders believe that it is the follower's responsibility to initiate contact with them. But the opposite is true. To be effective, leaders must be initiators. If they don't go to their people, meet them where they are, and initiate the connection, then 80 percent of the time no connection will be made.

4. Look for Common Ground

Anytime you want to connect with another person, start where both of you agree. And that means finding common ground. If you have developed good listening skills, as we talked about in Chapter 4, you'll probably be able to detect areas where you have common experience or views. Talk about hobbies, where you've lived, your work, sports, or children.

What you discuss isn't as important as your attitude. Be positive, and try to see things from the other person's point of view. Being open and likable is half the battle. As it's sometimes said, "All things being equal, people will do business with people they like. All things not being equal, they still will."

Sometimes even when you find common ground, you can face obstacles in the communication process. If you detect that people you're trying to connect with are tentative about your approaching them, then try to meet them on emotional common ground. An excellent way to do that is to use something called *feel, felt, found* to help them relate to you. First, try to sense what they *feel*, and acknowledge and validate the feelings. If you've had similar feelings in the past, then share with them about how you've also *felt* the same way before. Finally, share with them what you've *found* that has helped you work through the feelings.

Once you make it a regular practice to look for common ground with others, you'll find that you can talk to just about anybody and meet her where she is. And when you can do that, you can make a connection.

5. *Recognize and Respect Differences in Personality*

We are capable of finding common ground with others, but at the same time we need to acknowledge that we're all different. And that's one of the great joys of life, though we didn't always see it that way. An excellent tool for understanding other people is a book by John's friend Florence Littauer called *Personality Plus*. In it, she describes four basic personality types:

- *Sanguine:* desires fun; is outgoing, relationship oriented, witty, easygoing, popular, artistic, emotional, outspoken, and optimistic.
- *Melancholy:* desires perfection; is introverted, task oriented, artistic, emotional, goal oriented, organized, and pessimistic.
- *Phlegmatic:* desires peace; is introverted, unemotional, strong-willed, relationship oriented, pessimistic, and purpose driven.

- *Choleric:* desires power or control; is strong-willed, decisive, goal oriented, organized, unemotional, outgoing, outspoken, and optimistic.[3]

Just about everyone you try to connect with falls into one of these categories (or has characteristics from two complementary categories). For example, John is a classic choleric-sanguine. He loves to have fun, he is decisive, and he naturally takes charge in just about any situation. Jim, on the other hand, is melancholy-phlegmatic. He is an analytical thinker who's not driven by emotion, and he generally keeps his own counsel.

As you connect with others, recognize and respect their differences in motivation. With cholerics, connect with strength. With melancholics, connect by being focused. With phlegmatics, connect by giving assurance. And with sanguines, connect with excitement.

Playwright John Luther understood this point: "Natural talent, intelligence, a wonderful education—none of these guarantees success. Something else is needed: the sensitivity to understand what other people want and the willingness to give it to them." Pay attention to people's personalities, and do your best to meet them where they are. They'll appreciate your sensitivity and understanding.

6. Find the Key to Others' Lives

Industrialist Andrew Carnegie had an uncanny ability for understanding people and what was important to them. It's said that when he was a boy in Scotland, he had a rabbit that had a litter of bunnies. To feed them, Carnegie asked the neighborhood boys to collect clover and dandelions. In return, each boy got to name a bunny after himself.

Carnegie did something similar as an adult that showed his understanding of people. Because he wanted to sell his steel to the Pennsylvania Railroad, when he built a new steel mill in Pittsburgh, he named it the J. Edgar Thompson Steel Works after the president of the Pennsylvania Railroad. Thompson was so flattered by the honor that he thereafter purchased all his steel from Carnegie.

You don't have to be a Carnegie to connect with people. You just need to know what's important to them. Everybody has a key to his or her life. All you need to do is find it. Here are two clues to help you do it: To understand a person's mind, examine what he has already achieved. To understand his heart, look at what he aspires to do. That will help you find the key, and once you do find it, use it with integrity. Turn the key only when you have the person's permission, and even then use that key only for his benefit, not your own—to help, not to hurt.

7. Communicate from the Heart

Once you've initiated a connection with others, found common ground, and discovered what really matters to them, communicate to them what really matters to you. And that requires you to speak to them from your heart.

A young man with a brand-new degree in psychology was asked to deliver a speech to a group of senior citizens. For forty-five minutes he talked to them on how to live your twilight years gracefully. When the speech was over, an eighty-year-old woman came up to the young speaker and said, "Your vocabulary and pronunciation were excellent, but I must tell you one thing that you'll come to understand as you get older, you don't know what you're talking about!"

Being genuine is the single most important factor when communicating with others, whether one-on-one or before large audiences. No amount of knowledge, technique, or quick-wittedness can substitute for honesty and the genuine desire to help others.

Abraham Lincoln was well-known for communicating well with others, and at the heart of that skill was his ability to speak from the heart. In 1842, Lincoln addressed members of the Washington Temperance Society. During his speech titled "Charity in Temperance Reform," he made the following observation: "If you would win a man to your cause, first convince him that you are his sincere friend. . . . Assume to dictate to his judgment, or to command his action, or to mark him as one to be shunned and despised, and he will retreat within himself. . . . You shall no more be able to pierce him than to penetrate the hard shell of a tortoise with a rye straw."[4]

As you communicate with others to build connections with them, share from your heart and be yourself.

8. Share Common Experiences

To really connect with others, you have to do more than find common ground and communicate well. You need to find a way to cement the relationship. Joseph F. Newton said, "People are lonely because they build walls instead of bridges." To build bridges that connect you to people in a lasting way, share common experiences with them.

No one ever achieves alone what
he can do when partnering with others.

The two of us have enjoyed sharing experiences with others for years. For example, whenever John hires a new member of his executive staff, he always takes that person on the road with him to several of his conferences. He does that not only because he wants the new staff member to become familiar with the services the company offers to its customers, but also because they can travel together and get to know each other in a wide variety of settings. Nothing bonds people together like racing through impossible traffic in an unfamiliar city to get to the airport and then running with your bags down the concourse to scramble onto a plane at the last minute!

The common experiences you share with others don't have to be that dramatic (although adversity definitely brings people together). Share meals with people. Go to a ball game together. Take people out on a call or visitation with you. Anything you experience together that creates a common history helps to connect you to others.

A wonderful story of connection comes from the career of Jackie Robinson, the first African-American to play major-league baseball. Robinson faced jeering crowds, death threats, and loads of abuse in just about every stadium he visited while breaking baseball's color barrier. One day in his home stadium in Brooklyn, he committed an error, and immediately, his own fans began to ridicule him. He stood at second base, humiliated, while the fans jeered. Then shortstop Pee Wee Reese came over and stood next to him. He put his arm around Robinson and faced the crowd. The fans grew quiet. It's said that Robinson later claimed that Reese's arm around his shoulder saved his career.

Look for ways to build bridges with people within your influence, especially during times when they experience adversity. The connections you make will strengthen your relationships incredibly and prepare you for the journey you can take together.

9.   Once Connected, Move Forward

If you want to influence others, and you desire to get them moving in the right direction, you must connect with them before you try to take them anywhere. Attempting to do it before connecting is a common mistake of inexperienced leaders. Trying to move others before going through the connection process with them can lead to mistrust, resistance, and strained relationships. Always remember that you have to share yourself before you try to share the journey. As someone once observed, "Leadership is cultivating in people today, a future willingness on their part to follow you into something new for the sake of something great." Connection creates that willingness.

A challenge for any influencer is connecting with people from another culture. Jim has had a lot of experience in this area since he works with people in twenty-six countries. He found it particularly interesting working with people in the Eastern bloc countries formerly controlled by the Soviet Union:

When we first started working with people in Eastern Europe, it was really a unique experience. We had experienced very little exposure to their culture and values, and we found that things we accept in everyday business were foreign to people who had endured fifty years of Communist rule.

Most people in America have been raised on Judeo-Christian ethical and moral values. We often take that for granted, along with the benefits of free enterprise and capitalism. Our new friends in countries like

Poland, Hungary, and the Czech Republic, however, were used to surviving in a corrupt world of oppressive government, propaganda, and little-to-no-ethical teaching as we know it. Their environment led them to believe that success comes only to those who work *around* the rules and beat the cheaters at their own game. We found that many people embraced a success-at-any-cost mind-set and almost a pride in how cleverly they could break the rules.

We believed it was important to show these wonderful people that real success was possible only when a person behaved ethically and stood on the principles of integrity and trust. It seemed like a big job, but the people were smart, and we were working with some great young professionals who were hungry to learn the secrets of true success.

We began the process by doing everything we could to connect with people in those countries. In some ways, that has been one of our greatest challenges as influencers. But we were able to find a few key people, and we came alongside them as friends and mentors. We began navigating them through this new paradigm of ethical living and principle-centered business. And we invested a lot of time in getting to know them better and connecting with them on this worthwhile journey. Our goal was to give them tools to positively impact the people in their country.

This is still an ongoing journey for us. But whether we are working with people in Eastern Europe, mainland China, or another part of the world, we recognize that people are basically the same. Everyone wants to be successful and happy and is eager to learn from others who have gone ahead of them. But you can't make a significant impact in people's lives until you personally connect with them. Only then can you take them on a journey and really make a difference.

Jim and Nancy are making an impact that is being felt around the world. They understand that influence means relating to people, raising them up, and then turning them loose to reproduce themselves in others' lives. Connecting is a fundamental step in that process. But before people can go to the highest level and reproduce their influence in others, there is one more step they need to take: They need to be empowered. And that is the subject of the next chapter.

Influence Checklist

CONNECTING WITH PEOPLE

❏ **Measure your current connection.** How strong is your connection
with the top people whose lives you are influencing? Do you know the
key to each person's life? Have you established common ground? Are
there common experiences that bond you together? If your connection is not as strong as it could be, remember that it's your role to be
the initiator. Schedule time in the coming week to have coffee, share
a meal, or just chat with each person.

❏ **Connect at a deeper level.** If you've never spent any kind of meaningful time with your top people in a nonprofessional setting, schedule a time to do so in the coming month. Plan a retreat or a getaway
weekend, and include your spouses. Or take them to a seminar or conference. The main thing is to give yourselves opportunities to connect
on a deeper level and share common experiences.

❏ **Communicate your vision.** Once you've made a strong connection
with your people, share your hopes and dreams. Cast vision for your
common future, and invite them to join you on the journey.

CHAPTER 9

A Person of Influence . . .

EMPOWERS PEOPLE

MULTIPLY

MENTOR—*Empower*

MOTIVATE

MODEL

A big part of Jim's business includes meeting fairly often with some of his key leaders, and because they come from around the country and all over the world, he makes it a goal to schedule meetings in various locations. One place that has become a favorite of his and Nancy's over the years is Deer Valley near Salt Lake City, Utah. Recently, when they were there with some of their leaders, something interesting happened. Jim will tell you about it:

Deer Valley is really a beautiful setting. In the winter it's great for skiing, and in the summer it's got gorgeous forested mountains and meadows full of wildflowers. We really enjoy vacationing there and using it as a place to meet with some of our people.

This past year we spent time with a group of about ten couples at some condos in Deer Valley right on the ski slopes. We all had a wonderful time.

When we were ready to leave, we packed up our belongings and swung by the rental office to check out on the way to the airport. But as we worked to get our bill squared away, we discovered that one couple in our party had inadvertently left their room key in their condo.

"I'm going to have to charge you $25 for the lost key," the desk clerk said.

I have to admit I was a little surprised. We had been their customers for eight years. And we had spent thousands of dollars with them in the past week. "Look," I said, "I appreciate that you have a policy about missing keys, but the key is in their room. And if we were to go back and get it, we'd miss our flight. Can't you just forget the charge?"

"No," he said, "the rule is that I have to add the charge to your bill." Even when I reminded him of our history with their company and told him that I didn't feel good about the extra charge, he wouldn't budge. In fact, he got more rigid, and I got really irritated. As I stood there waiting, I calculated in my mind how much money we had spent there over the years, and I figured out that he was jeopardizing our $100,000 history with their company for a $25 key!

We finally left and paid the fee. On the way to the airport, Nancy and I talked about the incident, and I thought about how it really wasn't the desk clerk's fault. The problem was with the owner who had failed to train him properly.

"That kind of thing drives me crazy," she said. "Some people just don't get it. You know who's just the opposite of that?" she asked. "Nordstrom. They're unbelievable. I didn't tell you about what happened the other night before we left for Deer Valley. I went down to Nordstrom to get Eric a pair of pajamas. I picked out some that I knew he'd like, but I told the salesgirl that I needed the pants hemmed and that we were leaving on a trip early the next morning. She didn't blink and offered to have them done that night and drive them out to us at home.

"And that was the only thing I bought!" added Nancy. "It's not like I had spent a lot of money. She did that just for a pair of pajamas."

Stories of the excellent service at Nordstrom department stores have become legendary. Anyone who shops there can attest to it. Their employees are exceptional, because the company is built on the principle of *empowerment*. That philosophy of empowering employees is capsulized in the following brief statement that every employee receives when he or she begins working for the company:

Welcome to Nordstrom
We're glad to have you with
our Company.
Our number one goal is to provide
outstanding customer service.
Set both your personal and
professional goals high.
We have great confidence in your ability to achieve them.
Nordstrom Rules:
Rule #1: Use your good
judgment in all situations.
There will be no additional rules.
Please feel free to ask

> your department manager,
> store manager, or division general
> manager any question
> at any time.[1]

Nordstrom stores emphasize people, not policies. They believe in their people, they encourage them to achieve excellence, and they release them to do it. As Tom Peters said, "Techniques don't produce quality products or pick up the garbage on time; people do, people who care, people who are treated as creatively contributing adults." The managers and staff at that rental office in Deer Valley would benefit greatly from learning that lesson.

WHAT IT MEANS TO EMPOWER OTHERS

An English artist named William Wolcott went to New York in 1924 to record his impressions of that fascinating city. One morning he was visiting in the office of a former colleague when the urge to sketch came over him. Seeing some paper on his friend's desk, he asked, "May I have that?"

The act of empowering others changes lives,
and it's a win-win situation for you
and the people you empower.

His friend answered, "That's not sketching paper. That's ordinary wrapping paper."

Not wanting to lose that spark of inspiration, Wolcott took the wrapping paper and said, "Nothing is ordinary if you know how to use it." On that ordinary paper Wolcott made two sketches. Later that same year, one of those sketches sold for $500 and the other for $1,000, quite a sum for 1924.

People under the influence of an empowering person are like paper in the hands of a talented artist. No matter what they're made of, they can become treasures.

The ability to empower others is one of the keys to personal and professional success. John Craig remarked, "No matter how much work you can do, no matter how engaging your personality may be, you will not advance far in business if you cannot work through others." And business executive J. Paul Getty asserted, "It doesn't make much difference how much other knowledge or experience an executive possesses; if he is unable to achieve results through people, he is worthless as an executive."

> *When you empower people, you're not*
> *influencing just them; you're influencing*
> *all the people they influence.*

When you become an empowerer, you work with and through people, but you do much more. You enable others to reach the highest levels in their personal and professional development. Simply defined, empowering is giving your influence to others for the purpose of personal and organizational growth. It's sharing yourself—your influence, position, power, and opportunities—with others with the purpose of investing in their lives so that they can function at their best. It's seeing people's potential, sharing your resources with them, and showing them that you believe in them completely.

You may already be empowering some people in your life without knowing it. When you entrust your spouse with an important decision and then cheerfully back him up, that's empowering. When you decide that your child is ready to cross the street by herself and give her your permission to do so, you have empowered her. When you delegate a challenging job to an employee and give her the authority she needs to get it done, you have empowered her.

The act of empowering others changes lives, and it's a win-win situation for you and the people you empower. Giving others your authority isn't like giving away an object, such as your car, for example. If you give away your car, you're stuck. You no longer have transportation. But empowering others by giving them your authority has the same effect as sharing information: You haven't lost anything. You have increased the ability of others without decreasing yourself.

QUALIFICATIONS OF AN EMPOWERER

Just about everyone has the potential to become an empowerer, but you cannot empower everyone. The process works only when certain conditions are met. You must have:

Position

You cannot empower people whom you don't lead. Leadership expert Fred Smith explained, "Who can give permission for another person to succeed? A person in authority. Others can encourage, but permission comes only from an authority figure: a parent, boss, or pastor."

You can encourage and motivate everybody you meet. You can enlarge or help navigate for anyone with whom you have built a mentoring relationship. But to *empower* people, you have to be in a position of *power* over them. Sometimes that position doesn't have to be formal or official, but other times it does. For example, if we went to a restaurant to have lunch with you one day, and we weren't happy about how long it was taking to get our food, we could never empower you to go into the kitchen to fix our meal for us. We don't have that authority, so we certainly can't give it away to you. The first requisite of empowerment is having a position of authority over the people you want to empower.

Relationship

The second requirement for empowering people is having a relationship with them. Nineteenth-century writer Thomas Carlyle said, "A great man shares his greatness by the way he treats little men." Although the people you empower are not "little," they can be made to feel that way if you don't value your relationship with them.

It has been said that relationships are forged, not formed. They require time and common experience. If you have made the effort to connect with people, as we talked about in the previous chapter, by the time you're ready to empower them, your relationship should be solid enough for you to be able to lead them. And as you do, remember what Ralph Waldo Emerson wrote, "Every man [or woman] is entitled to be valued by his [or her] best moments." When you value people and your relationships with them, you lay the foundation for empowering others.

Respect

Relationships cause people to want to be with you, but respect causes them to want to be empowered by you. Mutual respect is essential to the empowerment process. Psychiatrist Ari Kiev summed it up this way: "If you wish others to respect you, you must show respect for them. . . . Everyone wants to feel that he counts for something and is important to someone. Invariably, people will give their love, respect, and attention to the person who fills that need. Consideration for others generally reflects faith in self and faith in others." When you believe in people, care about them, and trust them, they know it. And that respect inspires them to want to follow where you lead.

Commitment

The last quality a leader needs to become an empowerer is commitment. USAir executive Ed McElroy stressed that "commitment gives us new power. No matter what comes to us—sickness, poverty, or disaster, we never turn our eye from the goal." The process of empowering others isn't always easy, especially when you start doing it for the first time. It's a road that has many bumps and sidetracks. But it is one that's worth traveling because the rewards are so great. As Edward Deci of the University of Rochester stated, "People must believe that a task is inherently worthwhile if they are to be committed to it." If you need a reminder of the value of empowering others, remember this: When you empower people, you're not influencing just them; you're influencing all the people they influence. That's impact!

If you have authority in people's lives, have built relationships with them, respect them, and have committed yourself to the process of empowerment, you're in a *position* to empower them. But one more crucial element of empowering needs to be in place. You need to have the right attitude.

Many people neglect to empower others because they are insecure. They are afraid of losing their jobs to the people they mentor. They don't want to be replaced or displaced, even if it means that they would be able to move up to a higher position and leave their current one to be filled by the person they mentor. They're afraid of change. But change is part of empowerment—for the people you empower and for yourself. If you want to go up, there are things you have to be willing to give up.

If you're not sure about where you stand in terms of your attitude toward the changes involved with empowering others, answer these questions:

QUESTIONS TO ASK
BEFORE YOU GET STARTED

1. Do I believe in people and feel that they are my organization's most appreciable asset?
2. Do I believe that empowering others can accomplish more than individual achievement?
3. Do I actively search for potential leaders to empower?
4. Would I be willing to raise others to a level higher than my own level of leadership?
5. Would I be willing to invest time developing people who have leadership potential?
6. Would I be willing to let others get credit for what I taught them?
7. Do I allow others freedom of personality and process, or do I have to be in control?

8. Would I be willing to publicly give my authority and influence to potential leaders?
9. Would I be willing to let others work me out of a job?
10. Would I be willing to hand the leadership baton to the people I empower and truly root for them?

If you answer no to more than a couple of these questions, you may need an attitude adjustment. You need to believe in others enough to give them all you can and in yourself enough to know that it won't hurt you. Just remember that as long as you continue to grow and develop yourself, you'll always have something to give, and you won't need to worry about being displaced.

How to Empower Others to Their Potential

Once you have confidence in yourself and in the persons you wish to empower, you're ready to start the process. Your goal should be to hand over relatively small, simple tasks in the beginning and progressively increase their responsibilities and authority. The greener the people you're working with, the more time the process will take. But no matter whether they are raw recruits or seasoned veterans, it's still important to take them through the whole process. Use the following steps to guide you as you empower others:

1. Evaluate Them

The place to start when empowering people is to evaluate them. If you give inexperienced people too much authority too soon, you can set them up to fail. If you move too slowly with people who have lots of experience, you can frustrate and demoralize them.

Sometimes when leaders misjudge the capabilities of others, the results can be comical. For example, we read about an incident from the life of Albert Einstein that illustrates this point. In 1898, Einstein applied for admittance to the Munich Technical Institute and was rejected because he would "never amount to much." As a result, instead of going to school, he worked as an inspector at the Swiss Patent Office in Bern. And with the extra time he had on his hands, he worked at refining and writing his theory of relativity.

Remember that all people have the potential to succeed. Your job is to see the potential, find out what they lack to develop it, and equip them with what they need. As you evaluate the people you intend to empower, look at these areas:

- **Knowledge.** Think about what people need to know in order to do any task you intend to give them. Don't take for granted that they know all that you know. Ask them questions. Give them history or background information. Cast a vision by giving them the big picture of how their actions fit into the organization's mission and goals. Knowledge is not only power; it's empowering.
- **Skill.** Examine the skill level of the people you desire to empower. Nothing is more frustrating than being asked to do things for which you have no ability. Look at what people have done before as well as what they're doing now. Some skills are inherent. Others need to be learned through training or experience. Your job as the empowerer is to find out what the job requires and make sure your people have what they need to succeed.
- **Desire.** Greek philosopher Plutarch remarked, "The richest soil, if uncultivated, produces the rankest weeds." No amount of skill, knowledge, or potential can help people succeed if they don't have the desire to be successful. But when desire is present, empowerment is easy. As seventeenth-century French essayist Jean La Fontaine wrote, "Man is made so that whenever anything fires his soul, impossibilities vanish."

2. Model for Them

Even people with knowledge, skill, and desire need to know what's expected of them, and the best way to inform them is to show them.

People do what people see. A little parable about a farm boy who lived in a mountainous region of Colorado illustrates this point. One day the boy climbed to a high place and found an eagle's nest with eggs in it. He snatched one of the eggs while the eagle was away, took it back to the farm, and put it under a sitting hen who had a brood of eggs.

The eggs hatched one by one, and when the eaglet came out of his shell, he had no reason to believe he was anything other than a chicken. So he did everything that the other chickens did on the farm. He scratched around the yard looking for grain, he tried his best to cluck, and he kept his feet firmly planted on the ground, even though the fence around the pen wasn't more than several feet high.

That went on until he towered over his would-be siblings and his adopted mother hen. Then one day an eagle flew over the chicken yard. The young eagle heard its cry and saw it swoop down on a rabbit in the field. And at that moment, the young eagle knew in his heart that he wasn't like the chickens in the yard. He spread his wings, and before he knew it, he was flying after the other eagle. Not until he had seen one of his kind flying did he know who he was or what he was capable of doing.

The people you desire to empower need to see what it looks like to fly. As their mentor, you have the best opportunity to show them. Model the attitude and work ethic you would like them to embrace. And anytime you can include them in your work, take them along with you. There is no better way to help them learn and understand what you want them to do.

3. Give Them Permission to Succeed

As a leader and influencer, you may believe that everyone wants to be successful and automatically strives for success, probably as you have. But not everyone you influence will think the same way you do. You have to help others believe that they can succeed and show them that you want them to succeed. How do you do that?

- **Expect it.** Author and professional speaker Danny Cox advised, "The important thing to remember is that if you don't have that inspired enthusiasm that is contagious—whatever you do have is also contagious." People can sense your underlying attitude no matter what you say or do. If you have an expectation for your people to be successful, they will know it.

- **Verbalize it.** People need to hear you tell them that you believe in them and want them to succeed. Tell them often that you know they are going to make it. Send them encouraging notes. Become a positive prophet of their success.

- **Reinforce it.** You can never do too much when it comes to believing in people. Leadership expert Fred Smith has made it a habit to give people plenty of positive reinforcement. He says, "As I recognize success, I try to stretch people's horizons. I might say, 'That was terrific!' but I don't stop there. Tomorrow I might return, repeat the compliment, and say, 'Last year, would you have believed you could do that? You may be surprised at what you can accomplish next year.'"

Once people recognize and understand that you genuinely want to see them succeed and are committed to helping them, they will begin to believe they can accomplish what you give them to do.

4. Transfer Authority to Them

The real heart of empowerment is the transfer of your authority—and influence—to the people you are mentoring and developing. Many people are willing to give others responsibility. They gladly delegate tasks to them. But empowering others is more than sharing your workload. It's sharing your power and ability to get things done.

Management expert Peter Drucker asserted, "No executive has ever suffered because his subordinates were strong and effective." People become strong and effective only when they are given the opportunity to make decisions, initiate action, solve problems, and meet challenges. When you empower others, you're helping them develop the ability to work independently under your authority. W. Alton Jones offered this opinion: "The man who gets the most satisfactory results is not always the man with the most brilliant single mind, but rather the man who can best co-ordinate the brains and talents of his associates."

As you begin to empower your people, give them challenges you know they can rise to meet and conquer. It will make them confident and give them a chance to try out their new authority and learn to use it wisely. And once they've begun to be effective, give them more difficult assignments. A good rule of thumb is that if someone else can do a job 80 percent as well as you do, delegate it. In the end, your goal is to empower others so well that they become capable of meeting nearly any challenge that comes their way. And in time, they will develop their own influence with others so that they no longer require yours to be effective.

5. *Publicly Show Your Confidence in Them*

When you first transfer authority to the people you empower, you need to tell them that you believe in them, and you need to do it publicly. Public recognition lets them know that you believe they will succeed. But it also lets the other people they're working with know that they have your support and that your authority backs them up. It's a tangible way of sharing (and spreading) your influence.

John is especially talented at empowering people and publicly showing them his confidence, and he has an interesting story about one of his greatest successes in empowerment:

I mentioned in the last chapter that Dan Reiland has worked with me for fifteen years. When Dan first started with me, he was an intern, fresh out of graduate school. He had a lot of talent, but he still had some rough edges. I worked with him quite a bit—modeling, motivating, and mentoring him—and in a short time he grew to be a first-rate pastor.

In just a few years, he became one of my key players. When we had a new program that needed to be created and implemented, I frequently looked to Dan, empowered him to take on the task, and gave him my full confidence and authority. And he took care of it. Time after time, I'd give him a major project, he would work through the whole process, implement it, raise up leaders to run it, then come to me for another task. He continually worked himself out of a job.

In 1989, about six or seven years after Dan began working for me, I came to a point where I realized I needed to hire an executive pastor, a kind of chief administrative officer. And I knew right away that I wanted Dan to fill the position.

Now I knew that when you raise up a leader from within the ranks, there are often resentment and resistance from some of that person's colleagues. But I had a strategy. As I began to transfer my authority to Dan, I tried my best not to miss an opportunity to publicly praise him, show my confidence in him, and remind everyone that Dan spoke with my authority. As a result, the rest of the staff quickly rallied around him, and he was empowered as their new leader.

As you raise up leaders, show them and and their followers that they have your confidence and authority. And you will find that they quickly become empowered to succeed.

6.   Supply Them with Feedback

Although you need to publicly praise your people, you can't let them go very long without giving them honest, positive feedback. Meet with them privately to coach them through their mistakes, miscues, and misjudgments. At first, some people may have a difficult time. During that early period, be a grace giver. Try to give them what they need, not what they deserve. And applaud any progress that they make. People do what gets praised.

7.   Release Them to Continue on Their Own

No matter who you are working to empower—your employees, children, colleagues, or spouse—your ultimate aim should be to release them to make good decisions and succeed on their own. And that means giving them as much freedom as possible as soon as they are ready for it.

President Abraham Lincoln was a master at empowering his leaders. For example, when he appointed General Ulysses S. Grant as commander of the Union armies in 1864, he sent him this message: "I neither ask nor desire to know anything of your plans. Take the responsibility and act, and call on me for assistance."

That's the attitude you need as an empowerer. Give authority and responsibility, and offer assistance as needed. John and I have been fortunate to have been empowered by key people in our lives since we were kids. Probably the person who has been the most empowering in John's life is his father, Melvin Maxwell. He always encouraged John to be the best person he could be, and he gave him his permission and his power whenever he could. Years later as they talked about it, Melvin told John his philosophy: "I never consciously limited you as long as I knew what you were doing was morally right." Now that's an empowering attitude!

THE RESULTS OF EMPOWERMENT

If you head up any kind of organization—a business, club, church, or family—learning to empower others is one of the most important things you'll ever do as its leader. Empowerment has an incredibly high return. It not only helps the individuals you raise up by making them more confident, energetic, and productive, but it also has the ability to improve your life, give you additional freedom, and promote the growth and health of your organization.

Farzin Madjidi, program liaison for the city of Los Angeles, has expressed his beliefs concerning empowerment:

> We need leaders who empower people and create other leaders. It's no longer good enough for a manager to make sure that everybody has something to do and is producing. Today, all employees must "buy in" and take ownership of everything they're doing. To foster this, it's important that employees should make decisions that most directly affect them. That's how the best decisions are made. That's the essence of empowerment.

When it comes down to it, empowering leadership is sometimes the only real advantage one organization has over another in our competitive society.

As you empower others, you will find that most aspects of your life will change for the better. Empowering others can free you personally to have more time for the important things in your life, increase the effectiveness of your organization, increase your influence with others and, best of all, make an incredibly positive impact on the lives of the people you empower.

Jim recently received a letter from someone he has spent several years motivating, mentoring, and empowering. His name is Mitch Sala, and here's his letter:

Dear Jim,

I know you are in the process of writing a book on influence, and I feel the need to put pen to paper to express my deep respect and love for you and Nancy and tell you about the profound impact you've had on my life.

Your influence on me started before we even met when I listened to one of your tapes for the first time. Your vision, positive attitude, and committed faith were inspiring, and Nancy's ability to put life and its obstacles in proper perspective helped me to see my world in a new way.

As I observed you, I sensed an incredible depth of character in you. I admired that and wanted it myself. And it made me want to get to know you better, to develop our relationship. I had never really developed close friendships before, so that was new for me. You see, I grew up in Africa where my father ran a large sawmill in the forest. My older brother and sister were away at school, so I pretty much grew up without other kids around. I was kind of a loner. When I was eight, they sent me to traditional [boarding] school. It was good for my education, but bad for my self-image. It left me feeling like a loser.

As an adult, those feelings drove me to work hard and try to prove myself, but I still felt empty no matter what I did. And I was failing at the things that mattered to me most: being a good husband and father.

But you became an influence in my life at just the right time. You understood me and made me feel accepted despite my mistakes and failings. You've helped me to grow in my family life, financially, and spiritually. Everything has changed in my life.

Jim's positive influence has helped Mitch Sala change his life. Jim has taken him through the entire process. He has modeled a life of integrity to him. He has motivated and mentored him. He has empowered him. And over the years, Mitch has become a world-class influencer. Through his business enterprises and public speaking, Mitch touches the lives of hundreds of thousands of people every year in more than twenty countries around the world. And best of all, he is using his influence to raise up more leaders who are learning how to positively impact the lives of many more people. He has reproduced his influence in others, which is the subject of the final chapter of this book.

Influence Checklist

EMPOWERING PEOPLE

❑ **Give others more than just something to do.** If you lead a business, a department, a family, a church, or any other kind of organization, you are probably preparing to hand off some responsibilities to others. Before you officially start the process, carefully plan your strategy for passing the baton by using the following checklist:

Describe the task: _____

Name the person to whom you will give it: _____

What knowledge does the task require? _____

_____

Does the person have the required knowledge?   ❑ Yes ❑ No

What skills does the task require? _____

_____

Does the person have the skills required?   ❑ Yes ❑ No

Have you modeled how you want the job done?   ❑ Yes ❑ No

Have you given the person the authority and permission to succeed?

                                                    ❑ Yes ❑ No

Have you publicly given the person your confidence?   ❑ Yes ❑ No

Have you privately supplied the person with feedback? ❑ Yes ❑ No

Have you set a date to release the person to continue on his or her own?   ❑ Yes ❑ No

Repeat this process with every task you intend to delegate until it becomes second nature. Even when someone you empower is successful and established in performance, continue praising, encouraging, and showing your confidence publicly.

CHAPTER 10

A Person of Influence . . .

REPRODUCES OTHER INFLUENCERS

MULTIPLY—*Reproduce*

MENTOR

MOTIVATE

MODEL

At the beginning of this book, we told you about influencers and specifically about some of the people who have made an impact on our lives, people like Glenn Leatherwood, who was John's Sunday school teacher in seventh grade—and Jerry and Patty Beaumont, who took Jim and Nancy under their wing around the time Eric was born. Our lives have been filled with wonderful people of influence. But the greatest value has been added to our lives by people who not only influenced us, but also made influencers of us. In John's case, his father, Melvin Maxwell, has shaped and molded him the most, helping him to become an outstanding leader. And in the case of Jim, that place is probably held by Rich DeVos:

> I grew up in a great family. We had lots of love, even though there wasn't much money. My father's views on politics and economics were pretty liberal, and his advice to me was to go to college and get a good job. But when I was in my twenties, I heard Rich DeVos speak for the first time, and I was mesmerized. He introduced me to a whole new paradigm. He talked about free enterprise, the worth of the individual, dreams, freedom, and "compassionate capitalism." He also talked about his faith in God and encouraged people to live with integrity and passion. I had never before heard any philosophy that made so much sense as his simple message of personal achievement. I was forever changed.

Today, of course, Rich DeVos is one of the most influential businessmen in the world. He is a founder and past president of Amway; he owns the NBA's Orlando Magic; he is the president of Gospel Films and the DeVos Foundation; and he is frequently asked to give advice on business matters to presidents and other influential leaders. Jim has looked up to him as a leader and mentor, and over the years, he has come to call Rich his friend.

Rich DeVos understands the value of raising up leaders, people who are able to become influencers in their own right. In some ways, teaching others to become leaders is like handing off the baton in a relay race. If you run well but are unable to pass the baton to another runner, you lose the race. But if you run well, recruit and train other good runners, and learn to hand off the baton smoothly, you can win. And when it comes to influence, if you can do that process repeatedly, you can multiply your influence incredibly.

THE POWER OF MULTIPLICATION

In the work with people that the two of us have done, we've had to learn to hand off the baton. We never could have been successful if we hadn't. And now we want to hand it off to you. If you've moved successfully through the influence process, you've learned how to run the race. You understand how important it is for you to model integrity. You've learned to motivate people by nurturing them, having faith in them, listening to them, and giving them understanding. You understand that people really grow only when you mentor them. They have to be enlarged, navigated through life's difficulties, connected with, and empowered. Right now, you're running a good race. And if you've mentored others, you've got them running now too. But it's time to pass the baton, and if you don't get it into their hands, the race is over. They will have no reason to keep running, and the momentum will die with them.

That's why the reproduction phase of becoming a person of influence is so significant. Take a look at some benefits of creating leaders in your organization who are able to not only follow you but also influence others and raise them up:

- **Reproducing leaders raises your influence to a new level.** Anytime you influence people who either do not or cannot exercise influence with others, you limit your influence. But when you influence leaders, you indirectly influence all the people they influence. The effect is multiplication. (This idea is treated in greater depth in John's book *Developing the Leaders Around You.*) The greater your influence, the greater the number of people you can help.
- **Reproducing leaders raises the new leaders' personal potential.** Whenever you help others become better leaders, you raise the bar

on their potential. Leadership is the lid on a person's ability to perform and influence. A person acting independently who doesn't practice leadership can accomplish only so much, personally or professionally. But as soon as people understand leadership and start practicing leadership principles, they blow the lid off personal potential. And if they lead people who lead others, the potential for what they can achieve is almost limitless.

- **Reproducing leaders multiplies resources.** As you develop leaders, you'll find that your resources increase in value. You have more time because you can share the load and increasingly delegate authority. As the people on your staff learn leadership, they become wiser and more valuable as advisers. And as an added bonus, you receive personal loyalty from just about everyone you raise up.

- **Reproducing leaders ensures a positive future for your organization.** G. Alan Bernard, president of Mid Park, Inc., put the issue of raising up leaders into perspective: "A good leader will always have those around him who are better at particular tasks than he is. This is the hallmark of leadership. Never be afraid to hire or manage people who are better at certain jobs than you are. They can only make your organization stronger." Not only does it make an organization stronger when you develop leaders, but it gives that organization a strong future. If only a couple of people in the organization are capable of doing the leading, the organization can't flourish when they retire or anything happens to them. It may not even be able to survive.

John had the opportunity in 1995 to see exactly how an organization reacts when its leader leaves after equipping and empowering many strong leaders within it. Following fourteen years of leading and reproducing leaders at Skyline Wesleyan Church, John resigned from his position as senior pastor. He left so that he could devote himself full-time to INJOY, his organization that offers seminars and materials for leadership growth and personal development. And the result of his move? Skyline is doing very well. In fact, about a year after John left, he received a note from Jayne Hansen, an INJOY employee whose husband, Brad, was on staff at Skyline.

Dear John,

I was just thinking about Skyline and how it is really thriving since you've left . . . It's such an absolute TRIBUTE to the kind of leadership and lay ministry that you developed. We have a living example of the saying "practice what you preach" unfolding as we see the fruit of your labor. I can tell anyone without question that the principles you teach work. I can think of no greater honor than that a man pour his life into something, leave, and have it flourish! What a shame it would be to have a ministry die on the vine when one man leaves.

Thank you for pouring your life into us.

Your friend,
Jayne

Mentoring people and developing their leadership potential really can make a huge difference—for your organization, for your people, and for you.

AWAKEN THE REPRODUCER IN YOU

Everyone has the potential to multiply influence by developing and reproducing leaders. To awaken the reproducer in you, make the following principles a part of your life:

Lead Yourself Well

Being able to lead others begins with leading yourself well. You can't reproduce what you don't have. As entrepreneur and Chick-Fil-A restaurant chain founder Truett Cathy said, "The number one reason leaders are unsuccessful is their inability to lead themselves."

When we think about self-leadership, many qualities come to mind:

integrity, right priorities, vision, self-discipline, problem-solving skills, a positive attitude, and so forth. Desire and a game plan for personal development can help you cultivate these qualities, but the greatest obstacle to becoming a leader may be yourself. Psychologist Sheldon Kopp remarked about this problem: "All the significant battles are waged within the self."

If you haven't already put yourself on a program for growth and leadership development, start today. Listen to tapes. Go to conferences. Read enlightening books. (John's *Developing the Leader Within You* is an excellent primer for leadership development.) If you make personal growth your weekly goal and daily discipline, you can become a reproducer of leaders. Nineteenth-century theologian H. P. Liddon clearly saw this connection when he stated, "What we do on some great occasion will probably depend on what we already are; and what we are will be the result of previous years of self-discipline." Personal development pays dividends.

Look Continually for Potential Leaders

Former Notre Dame head football coach Lou Holtz said of a subject he knew well: "You've got to have good athletes to win, I don't care who the coach is." The same thing is true in your personal and professional lives. You need good people with leadership potential if you're going to reproduce leaders. Industrialist Andrew Carnegie emphasized that "no man will make a great leader who wants to do it all himself or get all the credit for doing it." Effective developers of people are always on the lookout for potential leaders.

It's said that "when the student is ready, the teacher appears." But it's also true that when the teacher is ready, the student appears. If you keep developing yourself as a leader, you will soon be ready to develop others. And if you want to be a great reproducer of leaders, you need to seek out and recruit the best people possible.

Put the Team First

Great developers of leaders think of the welfare of the team before thinking of themselves. J. Carla Northcutt, who receives John's monthly

INJOY Life Club tapes, stated, "The goal of many leaders is to get people to think more highly of the leader. The goal of a great leader is to help people to think more highly of themselves."

Bill Russell was a gifted basketball player. Many consider him to be one of the best team players in the history of professional basketball. Russell observed, "The most important measure of how good a game I played was how much better I'd made my teammates play." That's the attitude necessary to become a great reproducer of leaders. The team has to come first.

Do you consider yourself to be a team player? Answer each of the following questions to see where you stand when it comes to promoting the good of the team:

SEVEN QUESTIONS FOR A SUCCESSFUL TEAM ORIENTATION

1. Do I add value to others?
2. Do I add value to the organization?
3. Am I quick to give away the credit when things go right?
4. Is our team consistently adding new members?
5. Do I use my "bench" players as much as I could?
6. Do many people on the team consistently make important decisions?
7. Is our team's emphasis on creating victories more than producing stars?

If you answered no to a few of these questions, you may want to reevaluate your attitude toward the team. It has been said, "The ultimate leader is one who is willing to develop people to the point that they eventually surpass him or her in knowledge and ability." That should be your goal as you multiply your influence by developing leaders.

Commit Yourself to Developing Leaders, Not Followers

We believe that our country is experiencing a leadership crisis today. Not long ago, we saw an article in the *New Republic* that addressed the issue. In part it read, "Two hundred years ago, a little republic on the edge of the wilderness suddenly produced people like Jefferson, Hamilton, Madison, Adams, and others. Yet the total population was only 3,000,000 people. Today, we have over 200 million. Where are the great people? We should have 60 Franklins in a cover story on leadership. The search was in vain."

Ralph Nader, consumer advocate and founder of the Center for Responsive Law, declared, "The function of a leader is to produce more leaders, not more followers." Maybe two hundred years ago, people understood that better. But today, producing leaders isn't a priority for many people. Besides, developing other leaders isn't always easy or simple, especially for people who are natural leaders. As management expert Peter Drucker observed, "People who excel at something can rarely tell you how to do it."

That's why it's important for a person who wants to raise up other leaders to be committed to the task. We've said it before and we'll repeat it here: Everything rises and falls on leadership. When you raise up and empower leaders, you positively impact yourself, your organization, the people you develop, and all the people their lives touch. Reproducing leaders is the most important task of any person of influence. If you want to make an impact, you have got to be committed to developing leaders.

MOVING FROM MAINTENANCE
TO MULTIPLICATION

Many people live in maintenance mode. Their main goal is to keep from losing ground rather than trying to make progress. But that's the lowest level of living when it comes to the development of people. If you want to make an impact, you must strive to become a multiplier. Take a look at the five stages that exist between maintenance and multiplication, starting with the lowest:

1. Scramble

About 20 percent of all leaders live on the lowest level in the development process. They are not doing anything to develop people in their organization, and as a result, their attrition rate is off the charts. They can't seem to keep anyone they recruit. That's why we say they're in the scramble stage—they spend most of their time scrambling to find people to replace the ones they lose. You may know some small business owners who seem to stay in scramble mode. The morale in their organization stays low, and it doesn't take long for them to burn out from exhaustion.

2. Survival

The next stage in the development ladder is survival mode. In it, leaders do nothing to develop their people, but they do manage to keep the people they have. About 50 percent of all organizational leaders function this way. Their organizations are average, their employees are dissatisfied, and no one is developing personal potential. No one really benefits from this approach to leadership. Everyone merely survives from day to day without much promise or hope for the future.

3. Siphon

About 10 percent of all leaders work at developing their people into better leaders, but they neglect to build their relationships with their people. As a result, their potential leaders leave the organization to pursue other opportunities. In other words, they are siphoned off from the organization. That often leads to frustration on the part of the leader because other people benefit from their effort, and they must devote a lot of time to looking for replacements.

4. Synergy

When leaders build strong relationships, develop people to become good leaders, empower them to reach their potential—and are able to keep them in the organization—something wonderful happens. It's often called synergy, meaning that the whole is greater than the sum of its parts because the parts interact well together and create energy, progress, and momentum. An organization on the synergy level has great morale and high job satisfaction. Everyone benefits. Only about 19 percent of all leaders reach this level, but those who do are often considered the very best there are.

5.   Significance

Many people who reach the synergy level never try to go any farther because they don't realize they can take one more step in the development process, and that's to the significance level. Leaders on that level develop and reproduce leaders who stay in the organization, work to reach their potential, and in turn develop leaders. And that's where influence really multiplies. Only about 1 percent of all leaders make it to this level, but the ones who do are able to tap into almost limitless growth and influence potential. A handful of leaders continually functioning on the significance level can make an impact on the world.

HOW TO RAISE UP LEADERS
WHO REPRODUCE LEADERS

In an article published by the *Harvard Business Review,* author Joseph Bailey examined what it took to be a successful executive. In conducting his research, he interviewed more than thirty top executives and found that every one of them learned firsthand from a mentor.[1] If you want to raise up leaders who reproduce other leaders, you need to mentor them.

We've been told that in hospital emergency rooms, nurses have a saying: "Watch one, do one, teach one." It refers to the need to learn a technique quickly, jump right in and do it with a patient, and then turn around and pass it on to another nurse. The mentoring process for developing leaders works in a similar way. It happens when you take potential leaders under your wing, develop them, empower them, share with them how to become persons of influence, and then release them to go out and raise up other leaders. Every time you do that, you plant seeds for greater success. And as novelist Robert Louis Stevenson advised, "Don't judge each day by the harvest you reap but by the seeds you plant."

Now you know what it takes to become a person of influence, to positively impact the lives of others. Being an influencer means . . .

- modeling *integrity* with everyone you come into contact with.
- *nurturing* the people in your life to make them feel valued.
- showing *faith* in others so that they believe in themselves.
- *listening* to them so that you can build your relationship with them.
- *understanding* them so that you can help them achieve their dreams.
- *enlarging* them in order to increase their potential.
- *navigating* them though life's difficulties until they can do it themselves.
- *connecting* with them so that you can move them to a higher level.
- *empowering* them to become the person they were created to be.
- *reproducing* other leaders so that your influence continues to grow through others.

Over the years, Jim and I have worked hard to make this process more than a mere set of principles or method of working. We have sought to make investing in others a way of living. And as time goes by, we keep working to become better developers of people. Our reward is seeing the impact we make on the lives of other people. Listen to this story from Jim:

> One of the greatest things about becoming a person of influence is that you actually get to see the lives of others change before your eyes. I told you in the previous chapter about Mitch Sala, whom I got to see blossom into a person of impact. But what I didn't tell you is that Mitch has become more than just an influencer. He has gone through the entire development process himself and now is a great *reproducer* of influencers too.
>
> One of his greatest success stories is a man named Robert Angkasa. Robert is from Indonesia, holds an MBA from Sydney University, and used to work for Citibank, where he had risen to become a vice president in Jakarta by the time he was thirty years old.
>
> Robert has always worked hard. He put himself through school driving a taxi, working in restaurant kitchens, and cleaning stadiums after

concerts. But a few years ago, he met Mitch Sala. Mitch took Robert under his wing, motivated him, mentored him, and empowered him to become a person of influence.

Robert says, "The turning point in my life came when I met Mitch. At first, all I noticed was that he was a kind person. But the more time I spent with him, the more I realized that I wanted to be like him while still being myself. Mitch taught me that the way to success was through integrity and hard work. Today I am tasting the sweetness of a new life. I enjoy the financial security that's come from hard work, but more than that, I am becoming a better person. The pleasure that I get from helping others is enormous and gives me great satisfaction. I am a better person, husband, and family man. I owe a lot of who I am today to Mitch. He is a mentor, a friend, and a parent. I thank God every day for all his blessings that I've received through Mitch. And what I am trying to do now is be to others what he's been to me. I want to help others have a better life. The words *Thank you* don't seem sufficient, but they're the best words I can find."

Today Robert impacts the lives of thousands of people throughout Indonesia, Malaysia, China, and the Philippines. He is one of several key business leaders whom Mitch is now mentoring. And Robert's influence is continuing to increase daily.

My friend, you have the same potential as Robert Angkasa, Mitch Sala, or Jim Dornan. You can become a person of influence and impact the lives of many people. But the decision is yours. You can either develop your influence potential or let it remain unrealized. Jim gave the baton to Mitch. Mitch found Robert and taught him to run. He has successfully given the baton to Robert, and now he is running. There is one more leg—and the baton is ready. Now is your chance. Reach out your hand, take the baton, and finish the race that only you can run. Become a person of influence, and change your world.

Influence Checklist

REPRODUCING OTHER INFLUENCERS

❑ **Develop your own leadership potential.** The way to be prepared to teach others leadership is to continue developing your own leadership potential. If you haven't already put yourself on a personal plan for growth, start today. Select tapes, books, and magazines that you will review weekly for the next three months. Growth comes only if you make it a habit.

❑ **Find people with leadership potential.** As you continually enlarge and empower the people around you, some will emerge as potential leaders. Choose the person with the greatest potential for special mentoring, and talk to him or her about developing greater leadership skills. Proceed only if the person wants to be developed and agrees to mentor others in leadership in the future.

❑ **Teach the person to be a leader, not just perform tasks.** Give the person complete access to you, and spend lots of time modeling leadership. Devote time each week to increasing the person's leadership potential by teaching, sharing resources, sending him or her to seminars, and so forth. Do everything in your power to help that person reach his or her leadership potential.

❑ **Multiply.** When the person becomes a good leader, help him or her select someone to mentor in the area of leadership. Release them to work together, and find yourself a new potential leader so that you can keep repeating the process.

Notes

Introduction

1. John C. Maxwell, *Developing the Leader Within You* (Nashville: Thomas Nelson, 1993), 5–12.
2. Brad Herzog, *The Sports 100: The One Hundred Most Important People in American Sports History* (New York: MacMillan, 1995), 7.

Chapter 1

1. Stephen R. Covey, *The Seven Habits of Highly Effective People: Restoring the Character Ethic* (New York: Simon and Schuster, 1989).
2. Proverbs 22:1 NIV.
3. Donald T. Phillips, *Lincoln on Leadership: Executive Strategies for Tough Times* (New York: Warner Books, 1992), 66–67.
4. Bill Kynes, "A Hope That Will Not Disappoint," quoted in *Best Sermons 2* (New York: Harper and Row, 1989), 301.

Chapter 2

1. Everett Shostrom, *Man the Manipulator*.
2. *Bits and Pieces*.
3. Jack Canfield and Mark Victor Hansen, "All the Good Things," in *Chicken Soup for the Soul* (Deerfield Beach, FL: Health Communications, 1993), 126–28.
4. Arthur Gordon, "The Gift of Caring," in *A Touch of Wonder*.
5. Greg Asimakoupoulos, "Icons Every Pastor Needs," *Leadership*, fall 1993, 109.
6. Dennis Rainey and Barbara Rainey, *Building Your Mate's Self-Esteem* (Nashville: Thomas Nelson, 1993).

Chapter 3

1. 1 Samuel 17:32–37 NIV.

Chapter 4

1. Quoted by Fred Barnes in the *New Republic*.
2. David Grimes, (Sarasota, FL) *Herald-Tribune*.
3. Brian Adams, *Sales Cybernetics* (Wilshire Book Co., 1985), 110.
4. Eric Allenbaugh, *Wake-Up Calls* (Austin: Discovery Publications, 1992), 200.

Chapter 5

1. M. Michael Markowich, *Management Review,* cited in *Behavioral Sciences Newsletter.*
2. Art Mortell, "How to Master the Inner Game of Selling," vol. 10, no. 7.
3. Kent M. Keith, *The Silent Revolution: Dynamic Leadership in the Student Council,* (Cambridge, MA: Harvard Student Agencies), 1968.
4. Ecclesiastes 4:9–12 NIV.
5. Robert Schuller, ed., *Life Changers* (Old Tappan, NJ: Revell).

Chapter 6

1. Quoted in Og Mandino, *The Return of the Ragpicker.*

Chapter 7

1. *Saturday Review.*
2. Quoted in advertisement, *Esquire.*
3. Mortimer R. Feinberg, *Effective Psychology for Managers.*
4. "The Top Problems and Needs of Americans," *Ministry Currents,* January–March 1994.
5. Tim Hansel, *Holy Sweat* (Waco: Word, 1987), 134.
6. Ernie J. Zelinski, *The Joy of Not Knowing It All* (Edmonton, Alberta, Canada: Visions International Publishing, 1995), 114.
7. David Armstrong, *Managing by Storying Around,* quoted in *The Competitive Advantage.*

Chapter 8

1. Tom Peters and Nancy Austin, *A Passion for Excellence.*
2. Charles B. Ruth, *The Handbook of Selling* (Prentice-Hall).
3. Florence Littauer, *Personality Plus* (Grand Rapids: Revell, 1983), 24–81.
4. Carl Sandberg, *Lincoln: The Prairie Years.*

Chapter 9

1. *The Nordstrom Way,* 15–16.

Chapter 10

1. Joseph Bailey, "Clues for Success in the President's Job," *Harvard Business Review* (special edition), 1983.

About the Authors

JOHN C. MAXWELL is an internationally recognized leadership expert, speaker, and author who has sold over 12 million books. His organizations have trained more than one million leaders worldwide. Dr. Maxwell is the founder of Injoy Stewardship Services and EQUIP. Every year he speaks to Fortune 500 companies, international government leaders, and organizations as diverse as the United States Military Academy at West Point and the National Football League. A *New York Times, Wall Street Journal,* and *Business Week* best-selling author, Maxwell was one of 25 authors named to Amazon.com's 10th Anniversary Hall of Fame. Two of his books, *The 21 Irrefutable Laws of Leadership* and *Developing the Leader Within You,* have each sold over a million copies.

JIM DORNAN was educated at Purdue University in aeronautical engineering. He has successfully made the transition from aerospace to the world of global marketing and is president and owner of Network TwentyOne International. As an entrepreneurial visionary, he has taken the company into twenty-six countries around the world, with seminars attended by more than 100,000 people monthly. He is also co-founder, along with John Maxwell, of the non-profit EQUIP Foundation. Dornan's unique blend of logic and compassion has influenced and positively impacted the lives of nearly a million people worldwide.

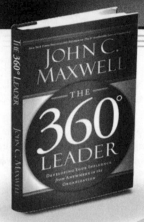

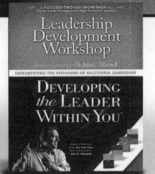
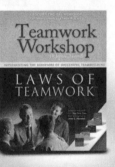